COLNE VALLEY

A HISTORY OF
A PENNINE LANDSCAPE

Rob Vincent

Huddersfield
Local
History
Society

Published by Huddersfield Local History Society
2021

© Copyright Huddersfield Local History Society

ISBN 978-0-9929841-3-7

Designed & Printed by Riasca

Front cover:
The Valley from Pule Hill

Back cover:
Looking up the Valley from Moorside Edge

Huddersfield
Local
History
Society

CONTENTS

FOREWORD

IF THESE DIFFICULT times have restricted and inhibited normal life in so many ways they have also encouraged everyone to think and act more creatively in how and where they use their time. For many lockdown has encouraged us, even socially distanced, to get our boots on and to explore. Indeed, it is probably true to say that more people have been getting out, walking and cycling, in our local landscape than for many years, if ever. The fresh air of our Pennine valleys and moor tops, even when wet, is a glorious antidote to the cabin fever so often induced by long periods of working from home. Significantly, certainly in my own case, it has also been an opportunity to get to know the place where I have lived all my life but have seldom explored as much as I might.

When the Huddersfield Local History Society's Publications Group was first offered a sight of the manuscript of Rob Vincent's *Colne Valley,* I was beginning to take the first steps in that exploration. Once read, there has been no turning back. With Heather, my wife and with members of the family and with friends when Covid regulations allowed, we have tramped all around the Valley and explored tracks and footpaths I never knew existed. Much of this has been due to Rob's infectious, enthusiastic and carefully researched writing and his very clear love of a place which, he freely admits, after forty years, has been hard to leave. The book is a love letter and a fond farewell.

Almost fifty years ago the then Colne Valley Society published its *Colne Valley Circular Walk* with a Foreword by no less a person than Phyllis Bentley. Some years later they followed that with *Countryside Guides* to the landscape around Marsden and Slaithwaite. Footpaths, tracks and possible routes for long or short walks were carefully devised and features of interest identified and explained. We would like to think that this twenty-first century re-visiting and extension of that pioneering work adds to an even deeper understanding of the Valley's landscape history.

Rob Vincent is the progenitor of this and we are hugely indebted to him for this work. However, bringing his manuscript to the point of publication has been a team effort and in this, with Steve Challenger, David Griffiths, Dave Pattern and others, we have been very well served. As the Huddersfield Local History Society we must apologise for extending our work beyond our usual boundaries but we hope that the good people of Golcar, Linthwaite, Slaithwaite and Marsden will accept this in the spirit intended and feel that Rob, as an adopted son of Bolster Moor, has done them and their Valley proud.

Cyril Pearce
Chair, Huddersfield Local History Society
August 2021, Golcar

ACKNOWLEDGEMENTS

THIS TEXT IS largely based on secondary sources. Many have been found by following threads that have taken me into the holdings of the West Yorkshire Archive Service, and then the British Library. Some have followed prompts from colleagues in the Huddersfield Local History Society (HLHS). I am particularly grateful to David Griffiths, Brian Haigh, Cyril Pearce and Milner Tomlinson, all of whom have pointed me at sources I would not otherwise have discovered. Dave Pattern's *Huddersfield Exposed* website has also been a rich source of prompts, and the texts now digitised on its pages have been a great help. They must have taken a great deal of effort – they are much appreciated.

Sadly one HLHS colleague, Brian Haigh, died just as this book was being prepared for printing. Brian was a stalwart colleague over many years, at Kirklees Council and in retirement. He gave me some strong leads and supportive advice as I worked on the text, and that was typical of him: always knowledgeable and always thoughtful and generous. A great loss.

Colleagues have also given me a great deal of help in shaping the text into a publishable form. I am grateful for the editorial and proof reading skills and patience of David Griffiths and Cyril Pearce in particular, and to Steve Challenger who improved many of the photographs, re-took those that were beyond redemption, and created much better versions of the maps than I had managed.

Colleagues from the Marsden History Group have also made a number of helpful suggestions, and the text draws on the group's research and publications in a number of places.

More generally, the network of Valley paths has benefitted from the labours of its two branches of the Walkers are Welcome network, and understanding of its way of life has been brought to life by the volunteers who run the Colne Valley Museum.

I am also grateful to several individuals and organisations that have generously allowed me to reproduce illustrations from their own works (see below), in particular the Huddersfield and District Archaeological Society for photographs taken from *The Romans Came this Way*, and the editors of the Roman Roads Research Association's Gazetteer for use of their materials. Both are to be found in the section describing the route of the Roman road from Castleshaw to Slack.

In so far as the text is based on primary sources, they are those found in the landscape itself. The pleasure of exploring that landscape has been greatly enhanced by sharing the challenges of navigating bogs on the tops and overgrown paths in the bottoms with my partner, Heather.

THIS BOOK IS DEDICATED to Tom, Kirstin, Isabel and Euan, and all the other families that have grown up at New Ing Farm over the years.

Rob Vincent
New Ing Farm
February 2021

ILLUSTRATION CREDITS

Photographs are by the author except where stated below. Other illustrations are reproduced with the permission of the following:

Brotherton Library, University of Leeds – fig. 9 (ref. YAS/MD358, redrawn by Cyril Pearce)
Stephen Challenger – figs. 4, 7, 14, 15, 18, 21, 30, 31, 33, 37, 38, 42–45, 52–56, 60, 62, 67, 75, 84
Huddersfield & District Archaeological Society – fig. 65
Huddersfield Exposed – fig. 49
Kirklees Image Archive – fig. 40
Roger Logue – fig. 39
National Library of Scotland (map base)/Stephen Challenger (annotation) – figs. 13, 17, 20, 29, 32, 47, 51, 80, 90
Ordnance Survey – fig. 3
Roman Roads Research Association – figs. 64, 66
Euan Vincent – fig. 57

INTRODUCTION

THIS IS A tribute to a strong and sinewy landscape.

Along the bottom of the Colne Valley run railways, canals and roads in threads of transport routes that connect West Yorkshire with Manchester and the Lancashire and Cheshire plains to the West. They run intertwined, like a bundle of arteries and veins, deep into the Pennines and then over or, in the case of the railway and the canal, under the high moors before dropping down into the Tame and Medlock valleys, which mirror their form and course on the other side of the hills.

The whole landscape shows evidence of the economy that has formed it – a distinctive combination of small scale farming and textile production. But the larger scale developments that followed the mechanisation of spinning, weaving and dyeing are all in the valley bottom. It is there that that the great stone mills that were part of the powerful Huddersfield textile, chemical and engineering industries of the late nineteenth and early twentieth century lie, and there too that developments continue to succeed each other, often partly overwriting the evidence of earlier histories. The landscape of the valley bottom changes perceptibly as each decade passes.

Above the valley bottom and below the moors the Colne Valley is a landscape of greens and greys: the greens of fields grazed by sheep and cattle; the greys of the drystone walls that enclose and order the fields, and of the houses and barns that stand, widely distributed, amongst them. Deep and steepsided valleys, cut by streams draining the moors, break up the field pattern. They are often accentuated by small woods hanging from their upper edges and following the water down. They are known locally as cloughs.

Here, on the valley sides and the tops, the steep slopes and low yields of Pennine farming have meant that change occurs slowly, even as centuries go by.

As a result the layers of history remain clearly legible in a landscape where the relationship between topography and human endeavour has always been powerful.

FIG. 1.
*Looking down the Valley,
from the side of Pule Hill,
above Marsden.*

The account that follows is based on what is visible in that landscape of the valley sides. It explores how what is visible came to be, and in so doing it seeks to tell the story of the economies and social structures of the generations that have both formed, and been formed by, their surroundings. It seeks to tell the landscape's history.

It follows the powerful model set by W.G. Hoskins in his ground-breaking book, *The Making of the English Landscape* (1955), and developed by generations of academics and amateurs ever since. I first read the book as a town planning student in the 1970s and, like many others, have found deeper enjoyment in looking at my surroundings, and trying to understand them, ever since.

But it is more particularly inspired by New Ing Farm, the home our family came to live in over thirty years ago. This stands just below the northern lip of the valley on land 'brought in' from the moor in the early 19th century – hence 'New Ing'. Its form is of the Colne Valley tradition – a property based on a mixed economy of cloth making and farming. The upper floor was once a weaving workshop accessed by a 'taking-in' door opening directly from the higher land at the back of the property. A long row of mullioned widows faces South-east, to allow as much light as possible to fall on weaving work that required sharp eyesight as well as dexterity and stamina. It has a small barn attached to the house, and a byre where a neighbour remembers milking a couple of cows during and just after the war. It has been carefully sited over a spring, which also fed a single storey stone dyehouse next to the property. It sits in a dip in the hillside so that the worst of the weather blows over its roof.

Its walls, floors and roof are all of stone hewn from a small quarry – a delph – some 100 yards away. It is a house built from the land on which it stands, and a property shaped by a way of life determined by the landscape around it.

The individual sections of this text tease out the threads from that landscape. It starts with the field patterns and walls that give a strong visual framework. It focuses next on the quarries and delphs from which their stones were derived.

It goes on to consider the influence of the Valley's dual economy of textile production and farming and the relationship of that economy with the distinctive, largely non-nucleated, settlement pattern.

It then turns to the Non-Conformist religious movements that were such a strong part of Valley life. Their strengths have left a rich heritage of chapels, churches and Sunday schools in the landscape. Their histories are entwined with the development of a society of self-reliant and free-thinking families – a society with a tradition of political as well as religious dissent.

A section on the networks of connections in the Valley follows – tracks, highways, canal, and railway. The last of the individual sections considers one further strong visual element in the Valley's landscape – its reservoirs.

The text considers each thread in turn, setting out the way in which each set of features was formed as the economy and the society of the Valley evolved, and then trying, briefly, to summarise their significance in the landscape and its history.

A brief final section aims to weave the threads back together into one cloth – the fabric of the scene as experienced by anyone who looks around and ponders the landscape history of the Valley.

FIG. 2.
New Ing Farm. The track to the upper left leads to the delph from which its stones would have been quarried.

A NOTE FOR READERS

THE PHOTOGRAPHS AND maps that illustrate this book are important to its message – it is as much about enjoying the features in the landscape as it is about their particular histories.

With that in mind, readers may want to locate the features illustrated, don their walking boots, and get out in the Valley to take a look. The maps at the end of each section are there to pinpoint the most significant locations. With the exception of the initial map opposite, of the area covered, which is based on the current OS 1:25,000 map, the location maps use as a base the database of OS 7th edition one inch to the mile maps maintained as an online resource by the National Library of Scotland.

Where features are not easily found, even with use of the 1:25,000 OS maps, an Ordnance Survey grid reference is supplied in the photograph caption.

The spellings of place names evolve over time. Where the text refers to historic references the original spellings have been used. More generally the spelling that seems most common has been used, although many still have alternative forms.

THE COLNE VALLEY

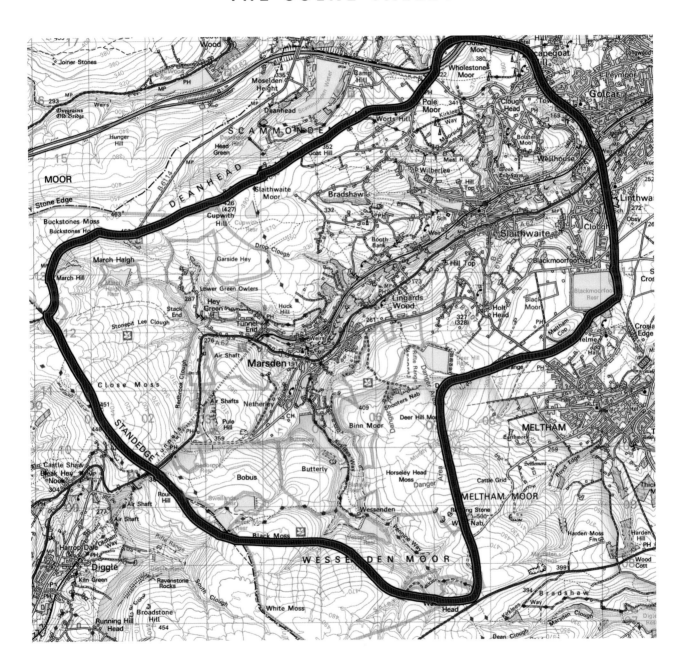

FIG. 3. *(Crown Copyright. Ordnance Survey licence no. 96921730)*

FIELD PATTERNS
AND WALLS

IT IS THE field pattern that provides a matrix for the Colne Valley landscape. The scenery is constantly changing: hourly as the Pennine weather blows through with curtains of rain, banks of mist, and shafts of sunlight; seasonally as fresh grass grows, beasts graze, hay and silage are cut, and the colours of the pastures fade away into the winter. But these changes play across a form that is ordered and constant. The field pattern changes very slowly as centuries pass.

The sense of long-established order in this pattern is part of the appeal of the Valley, but closer study soon reveals a layering within the pattern. Around the farmhouses and hamlets on the shoulders that are to be found half way up the valley sides are small irregular fields. Much of the rest of the lower ground is a pattern of larger fields, sometimes running up to a long head-wall that divides the farmland from the moor. In one large area there is a much more regular pattern of fields laid out with straight lines and right angles. These are Parliamentary enclosure fields from the early nineteenth century.

The fundamental framework of the Valley landscape is best understood by considering the evolution of each element in the field pattern in turn, and the distinct characteristics of their field shapes and wall styles.

FIG. 4.

Looking down Crimble Clough from Wholestone Hill. The nineteenth century Golcar Enclosure fields on the top of Bolster Moor, to the upper left, contrast with the older field patterns on the valley sides and the woods hanging over the steep clough that runs down to the valley floor.

Early landscape and the evolution of the first field patterns

> ... standing on the edge of the moors almost anywhere along these valleys, the Calder, Colne or their main tributaries, one can look out across a unique landscape, often of great though not conventional beauty. The scene is an epitome of long years and even of centuries of social and economic evolution and one can strip away century after century of accretion until the naked Pennine scene of magnificent high plateau and deep-cut valleys and ravines is all that remains.
>
> Arthur Raistrick (1970)

The Colne Valley leads from the broad Yorkshire acres deep into the Pennines. It is the eastern part of a major crossing that passes over the moors at one of their narrowest sections and then drops down into the Tame and Medlock valleys to the West and then on into Lancashire and Cheshire beyond. It will have been used as a route across the backbone of the country in pre-historic times, and early settlers have left some traces on the hills.

The most significant of these is perhaps the Bronze Age (3000 b.c.e. – 1200 b.c.e.) burial site on the crest of Pule Hill. There is little to see on the surface: just a low mound which is easy to miss, but the site has fine long views to both the East and the West. Excavations in 1896 found evidence of burial chambers cut into the rock, urns containing burnt remains within them, and a scattering of worked flints (Petch, 1924). The flints seem to have come from the Mas d'Azil workshop, which operated in a much earlier period in the foothills of the French Pyrenees – a reminder of the reach of the trading patterns of early communities.

The *West Yorkshire Archaeological Survey* (Faull and Moorhouse, 1981) notes a scatter of other sites. It records three older, Mesolithic, sites on Slaithwaite Moor, and one at Blake Lea. There is evidence of flint working at Cupwith Hill, and a polished stone axe was found at Meal Hill.

But it is March Hill, close to the current A640 as it crosses the Pennine watershed North of Marsden, that has offered up the most evidence of flint working. Such was the enthusiasm for finding worked tools in the early nineteenth century that little of the current hillside is undisturbed ground. That story, a careful analysis of the evidence that can still be retrieved from excavation and the re-assessment of earlier finds, and some thoughtful speculations on their implications for the use of the hill for encampments in Mesolithic times, are set out by Spikins (2003). She traces the flint that was being worked on March Hill back to the Yorkshire and Lincolnshire Wolds.

In other parts of Yorkshire, notably around Grassington, the pattern of Bronze Age fields themselves is still visible in the landscape. Nothing similar is now visible in the Colne Valley, but there is still evidence of a field system belonging to a medieval vaccary, or cattle ranch, in the Wessenden Valley.

FIG. 5.
Vaccary wall, in fields near Norland.

Vaccary in the Wessenden Valley

Vaccaries were medieval cattle ranches, owned by feudal lords or the monasteries of the twelfth to fifteenth centuries, but often some distance from them. At Norland near Sowerby Bridge, just over the watershed from the Colne Valley, there is a distinctive vaccary wall of stone slabs set vertically in the ground.

The walls of the Wessenden vaccary are also distinctive, but much messier. In several places they take the form of 'consumption' walls: great accumulations of stones cleared from the fields and piled along their edges. Others, also built from cleared field stones, wind up the hillside along ancient tracks. They have bases made of massive boulders, or outcrops of bedrock, under upper levels made without courses and with stones laid without fillers between the faces. These too are ancient, and quite possibly early medieval.

Walls are almost impossible to date accurately, not least since those which have had a sustained purpose will have seen sections rebuilt throughout their existence. But the sources of their stones, the lines they follow, and the features of their construction all give broad indications of age. A good summary is set out in Heginbottom (1993).

The vaccary may be one of the six located in Marsden recorded in a 1322 document (WYAAS Historic Environment Record). An area of ancient woodland can be found on the same steep hillside above the Butterley Reservoir. Both are described in a fascinating study by Christopher Atkinson, prepared in 2017 for the Wessenden Valley Woodland Project, which can

FIG. 6.
Walls in an area that was part of the Wessenden vaccary (SE 0529 1000).

be found online at *www.celebrate-our-woodland.co.uk*. He used LiDAR (a laser-based topographical surveying technique) to find outlines of a vaccary field pattern.

He also noted the names of Booth and Booth Laithe along the upper edge of the fields: names that originally belong to herdsmen's shelters, but came to be used to refer to the areas of tenanted land around them. (See Seidel, 2013, for the evidence of the booths in the Marsden area.)

Late medieval assarts

Just to the South of the vaccary, and also picked out on in the LiDAR scans, is the woodland which is registered as 'ancient' in the *West Yorkshire Archaeological Service Historic Landscape Categorisation, Kirklees* (2017). ('Ancient' here means existing from some period between 1066 and 1429.) This woodland, now mainly made up of oak and birch, would have covered the whole of the valley, and indeed much of the South Pennines, until early clearances by farmers settling in the area. Their clearances are known as 'assarts', a word with a Latin root, meaning 'out of the weeds', according to the *Oxford English Dictionary* (OED).

Although the Wessenden vaccary is made distinct by its monastic connection, assarts are to be found along the length of the valley. Nigel Smith's work on *Pennine Settlement and Field Patterns* (2013) suggests that they became more frequent following the break-up of vaccaries that accompanied the dissolution of the monasteries in the fifteenth century, and continued, on increasingly higher ground, into the seventeenth century.

FIG. 7.
Assarted field pattern at Owlers, above Marsden (owlers is the Old English version of alders – suggesting the woodland within which the original assart was established).

FIG. 8.

Walling below Badger Gate, on the South side of the valley (SE 0663 1250).

They mostly lie on the Colne Valley's distinctive shoulders – those relatively flat areas which a combination of geology and erosion have left half way up the slopes between the river and the moors. It is on these shoulders that the earliest farms were established, and where the distinctive patterns of assarted fields are still a strong element in the landscape.

Assarts were often oval in form, perhaps because a circular or oval boundary is the most energy-efficient way of establishing a clearing in the forest. They were first formed around a central farm, but were often extended by further intakes of small fields and further houses, perhaps as families expanded through subsequent generations. The result is a slow growth of a cellular field pattern, which looks organic rather than set out on planned lines. Their form is best appreciated by looking across from the opposite side of the valley. The field pattern at Owlers, to the North-west of Marsden, is a particularly striking example.

The fields on the shoulder of the valley to the South of Marsden, below the Binns, are another example, as are the fields above Redbrook Clough as it climbs up to the West of the village. There are several further areas which suggest early assarts on the North side of the valley, and here too you can find walls built on an orthostat base. (Orthostats are large stones set vertically.) These are characteristic of medieval walling. There are several examples of such walling along the valley sides – along Bradshaw Lane and below Great Edge on the North side, and below Badger Gate on the South.

The Brotherton Library at Leeds University contains a late eighteenth century map of Hey Farms near Linthwaite (catalogue number YAS/MD358) which shows what is probably an oval assart amongst a pattern of more rectangular fields developing around it as further land was taken into use from the moor.

FIG. 9.

Hey Farms – sketch based on a late eighteenth century map showing a central oval, perhaps the original assart, amidst a pattern of rectangular fields. Each field has its own name describing its location or vegetation. 'Hey' is a South Pennine term for a shared rough pasture.

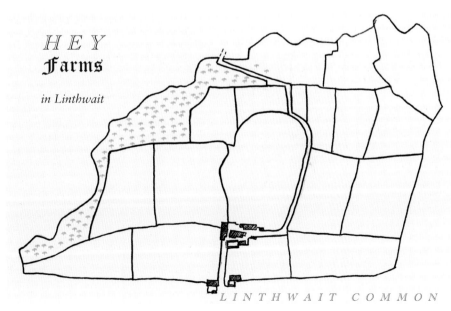

HEY
Farms

in Linthwait

LINTHWAIT COMMON

11

If that is right it is a typical pattern. Heginbottom (1993) suggest that early assarts in the Calder Valley date from the thirteenth century. Their creation was stalled by the Black Death in the mid-fourteenth century, but then gained momentum as further land was taken-in throughout the fifteenth and sixteenth centuries. These assarts were often circular or oval, but after 1600 land adjoining the original assarts was added, and the additional fields were more often roughly rectangular, as they are at Hey Farms. More land was taken in as new generations sought their own livelihoods. The pattern reached along the terraces, up towards the higher land, and down towards the heavily-wooded valley bottoms.

The track round the East side of the Hey Farms assart is still there. The walk along it and on down to Bradley Brook takes you through a landscape little changed from the late-eighteenth century, and probably from the seventeenth century or earlier.

It is this pattern of small, roughly rectangular, fields that shapes much of the landscape on both sides of the valley between the high natural terraces and wooded cloughs and the valley bottom. Where the land is steepest and least accessible from the roads, the fields and walls seem little changed since their sixteenth or seventeenth century origins. The walls are made from un-worked stone and the gates are narrow.

The now derelict farm buildings known as Nathans and Old Ash, below Hollins Lane and Badger Hey on the South side of the valley, also seem little changed. The field walls are of unworked stone, and follow natural courses along the contours. Many seem very old, perhaps also once part of medieval assarts. The field entrances are narrow, and there are posts worked to hold spars rather than hinged gates – a seventeenth century characteristic.

FIG. 10.
Wall of massive cleared field stones, above derelict farm below Badger Hey. Marked as Rollinsons on the OS 1st edition 6 inch map of 1854, and Old Ash on the 25 inch map of 1890 (SE 0647 1250).

FIG. 11.
Seventeenth century post,
showing slots for spars
rather than a hinged gate.

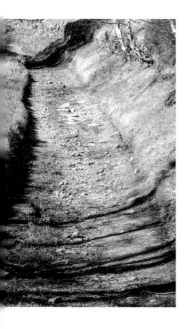

FIG. 12.
A Gate to the moor.
This one is near Holt Head.

Winding up through these field are walled tracks, leading from the hamlets on the valley sides up to the rough grazing above. These are the 'Gates', or 'Yates' in the local dialect, that were used to take cattle up to the summer grazing. Under the medieval township laws each farm would have had a 'stint', entitling the family to graze a number of beasts during the summer months.

Upkeep of the sixteenth and seventeenth century landscape – the record in the Manorial Rolls

Anyone taking an interest in the Valley soon comes across the work of the Freeman sisters, Margaret and Mary. They were the daughters of Edgar Freeman, a solicitor practising in Slaithwaite. After university they had long professional careers, as a teacher and as a solicitor respectively, before retiring together to the village in the 1970s and becoming local historians. One of their great contributions to local history was to translate the sixteenth and seventeenth century Court Rolls of Slaithwaite cum Lingards, part of the Dartmouth estates since the eighteenth century, from the Latin.

The rolls record the proceedings of the Manorial Court meetings, which occurred once a year in the 1540s, but less frequently thereafter. The earliest record is from 1524, and the last in 1682, but there are several long gaps which suggests missing records rather than a lack of meetings. The tenants assembled for each court hearing are recorded, as are the absences. Various transgressions are listed and adjudicated, and fines are raised. Various 'requirements' are declared, sometimes of individual tenants and sometimes of the community as a whole.

Many of the transgressions in the earlier records relate to the unauthorised taking of wood from the forest. There would have been a general right to collect fallen branches, but not to chop boughs from living trees. Hence, in 1524, nine individuals (five Sykes, a Haigh, a Firth, two Shaws) were amerced for taking greenwood. (An amercement was a fine.) In 1528 James Sikes, William Sikes, and James Sikes (son of William) were amerced for cutting down ten oaks to make their houses – a reminder that in this period most houses were timber and turf constructions. The illegal taking of peat for heating homes was also a common offence.

A significant number of interventions in the sixteenth century also related to the maintenance of watercourses: in 1549 there were Court interventions over a blocked water course at Moregate, a requirement to straighten the watercourse at Morecote, and one to clear ditches at Car Inge. Those who live on the Colne Valley hillsides even now will understand the nuisance caused by neighbours higher up the slopes who fail to attend to their springs and drainage channels.

There are frequent injunctions over the maintenance of tracks and 'yates'. Some are requirements that relevant tenants look to the proper maintenance of tracks for which they are responsible. Many edicts, particularly in the seventeenth century records, are restrictions on the use of particular routes, often following petitions from tenants who have evidently been exasperated by the passage of beasts across their land.

Many of the general requirements set out by the courts relate to the control of animals. One of the earliest, from 1541, is that:

> … each of the inhabitants should have his pigs ringed between the feast of Purification of the Blessed Mary and that of Michael the Arcangel under pain of 8d each. And they should have their pigs yoked between the Feast of the Annunciation & that of Michael Arcangel under pain of 8d each. (The two periods run from early February and from mid-June to late September.)

The place names recorded in the rolls, often identifying the homes of those sitting as the court rather than those affected by its decisions, provide strong evidence of the fifteenth century settlement pattern. (A later section puts this settlement pattern into the context of the linked textile and farming economies.)

The family names make clear the stability of the community, and its economy. There are Sikes/Sykes, Heys, Haighs, Mellors and Shaws – all common Valley names to this day.

Copyhold tenancies

The nature of land holdings in the Colne Valley has had a major effect on the care with which the landscape has been developed and managed. It is an area where the use of copyhold tenancies was adopted relatively early. In 1499 Marsden tenants successfully petitioned Henry VII for their use (see the work of the Marsden History Group on probate inventories set out by Hazel Seidel's book *Laithes and Looms, Cows and Combsticks* (2013)). 'Copy' here refers to tenants' rights being recorded in a copy of the entry for the piece of land in the manorial roll. The key point was that such rights were inherited by the tenant's children on death – a significant development from the insecurities of medieval villein status. Where there was a secure and inheritable right to the land the motivation to improve it, to invest in its buildings, and to maintain its walls and water courses was high. The quality of the infrastructure in the landscape reflects that. Arguably copyhold rights also gave the tenants the sense of security and independence that gave rise to the household-based enterprises of the Valley's dual economy which developed from the sixteenth century onwards.

Field patterns by the end of the eighteenth century

Throughout the seventeenth and eighteenth centuries more and more land was taken in as the Colne Valley economy developed. The woollen trade strengthened. The valley bottoms began to develop.

Fields from this period tend to be rather larger, and often form a more regular pattern. They were planned on maps, drawn up by surveyors commissioned by the owners of the landed estates, rather than just created around natural features on the ground.

The West Yorkshire Archive contains estate and township maps which provide a picture of the landscape at the end of the eighteenth century: the map of the Radcliffe Estate in Linthwaite and Golcar of 1786, the 1805 survey of the Dartmouth Estate in Lingards and Slaithwaite, and the John Johnson map of Marsden in Almondbury of 1801.

Where the estates extended down to the valley bottom many of the eighteenth century fields are now lost beneath nineteenth century and later developments. Where they extended up towards the flatter land below the moors, many of them have now been amalgamated into larger fields more suitable for modern farm machinery. But much of the landscape in between is little changed.

The areas marked in the map (fig. 13) show extensive tracts of land on the slopes of the valley between Slaithwaite and Marsden with field boundaries that are essentially the same as those mapped for the estate surveys. They include those picked out and illustrated above as having characteristics that suggest little change since late-medieval times. It is a landscape that the Colne Valley radicals of the early and mid-nineteenth century, the Luddites and the Chartists, would have recognised.

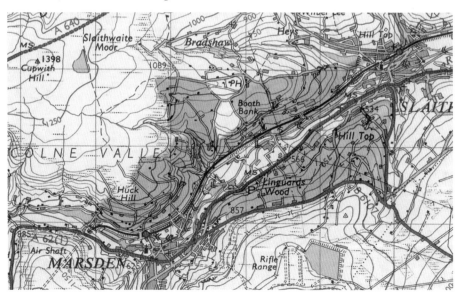

FIG. 13.

Areas of the valley sides with field boundaries little changed since the end of the eighteenth century.

Pinfolds and sheep folds

There are several Pinfold Lanes in the Valley, and one extant pinfold. Pinfolds were enclosures for keeping stray animals, usually sheep in the Pennines. The word seems to go back to the thirteenth century, and pinfolds were still in use in the eighteenth century.

The pinfold that still remains in the Valley, restored quite recently but now half-hidden in the undergrowth, is at Ainley Place, one of the hillside hamlets that existed in the fifteenth century. It is one of 200 that are still visible across the country, many of them rectangular but typically circular in Yorkshire.

According to Dorothy Beaumont's *Notes on the Dartmouth Estate records* (1985) the Pinder (who managed the pinfold) in the early nineteenth century was one Jimmy Pyzard, who lived at Burnt Platts, on the moor above the hamlet.

Other Pinfold Lanes are to be found between Pole Moor and Scammonden, at Clough Head, and at Paddock Brow. In Marsden what is now Warehouse Hill is shown as Pinfold Lane on the 1801 Survey Map. The Scammonden pinfold, just beyond the northern edge of the Colne Valley, is still to be found, near to Shaw Clough.

The annual rhythm of sheep farming is punctuated by gathering the sheep in. Sometimes this is to move them but also to inspect them, to collect ewes to be put to the tup, to mind the pregnant ewes through lambing, to separate the lambs at the end of the season. Gathering sheep requires a small enclosure into which they can be driven by farmer and dog – often an enclosure of metal hurdles these days, but before that a small stone enclosure at the edge of the grazing.

FIG. 14.
*Pinfold at Ainley Place
(SE 0653 1488).*

FIG. 15.
*Sheep fold below March Hill
(SE 0205 1332).*

Most of the early sheep folds of the Valley have fallen back into the hillsides, but there are two fine examples close to March Haigh reservoir, to the North of Marsden, and one high in the Wessenden Valley. These are highly functional shapes – the subdivisions allow the sorting and separation of the beasts.

Large scale enclosure in the late eighteenth and nineteenth centuries

The late eighteenth century saw an agricultural revolution in England, following innovations in farming techniques, partly promoted by 'Turnip' Townshend and his followers, and driven forward by landowners seeking greater control over their holdings and increased incomes. Commons and wasteland were enclosed, drains laid, fields limed, and crop rotation introduced. Williamson (2002) draws attention to the passing of upland landscapes into private ownership on a vast scale through the eighteenth and nineteenth centuries.

In the Colne Valley the economic and social changes that drove the Luddite cause are evident in the changes that occurred in the landscape as domestic weaving and small dye works and shearing sheds were supplanted by the industrial-scale mills of the valley bottom through the second half of the nineteenth century. The dual economy of the hillside small holdings gave way to larger farms supplying milk, eggs and meat to the growing populations in the terraces below.

Fields were agglomerated into a larger-celled, more planned, landscape, and new enclosures took in what had been rough grazing on the higher land. Much of the current landscape above the lower valley sides was created during this period. The field boundaries are straight, no longer following contours and natural features but conforming to patterns drawn on a plan. The walls are built with regular courses of sawn stone from larger, more mechanised quarries. Gateways are larger, allowing machinery as well as beasts to enter. Some of the nineteenth century enclosure areas are strikingly well set out, such as the area known as Stone Folds, on the moor edge to the North of Marsden.

Parliamentary enclosures

It was during this period that Parliamentary Acts confirming enclosure proposals became common across England as a whole. The case for enclosure in the West Riding was made forcibly in the *General view of the Agriculture of the West Riding of Yorkshire* set out by Rennie, Brown and Shirreff in their report of 1794:

> Upon the higher grounds, there are immense tracts of waste, which are generally common to the contiguous possessors, and pastured by them with cattle and sheep. Some of these are stinted pastures, but the greatest part are under no limitations: the consequences of which are [...] – the grounds are oppressed, the stock upon them starved, and little benefit derived from them by the proprietors.

> There are the lands adjoining the manufacturing towns. The greatest part of the ground is there occupied by persons who do not consider farming as a business, but regard it only as a matter of convenience. The manufacturer has his little inclosure, wherein he keeps milk cows for supporting his family, and horses for carrying his goods to market, and bringing back raw materials.

> The advantages of inclosure are great and manifold. The rent to the landlord is immediately raised at least one fourth; and how could this be paid if more corn and grass were not produced than by open field management? They enable the farmer to practise a more improved system, by introducing the grass husbandry in all its perfection, and the improvement of all kinds of stock is necessarily great.

> These things are so obvious to every person acquainted with the subject, or who will taketh trouble to examine the present state of the common fields and wastes, that we would hardly have mentioned them, if some popular writers, particularly the late Dr Price, had not attempted to show that the number of the people in this island has decreased, and assigned inclosing as the principal cause.

FIG. 16.
Nineteenth century walls at Stone Folds, on the North side of the Valley above Marsden. The spoils heaps of quarry workings can be seen above the higher fields (SE 0437 4129).

The Dr Price in their sights was Richard Price, who had published an *Essay on the Population of England* in 1780. He had compared the number of houses recorded for the late seventeenth century Hearth Tax, about 1.3 million, with those recorded for the Window Taxes a century later – under one million. But in doing so he had used data sets that were based on incompatible criteria, and he thus perhaps deserved the scorn heaped on him in the 1794 report.

The Napoleonic Wars gave further cause for improving agricultural yields, in part through enclosure of the wastes. Here is Sir John Sinclair, President of the Board of Agriculture, writing in 1803:

> We have begun another campaign against the country [of France]. .. why should we not attempt a campaign also against another foe, I mean the hitherto unconquered sterility of so large a proportion of the kingdom? . . . Let us not be satisfied with the liberation of Egypt, Malta, but let us subdue Finchley Common; let us conquer Hounslow and force Epping Forest to submit to the yoke. (Williams, 1970)

Parliamentary enclosures went on at pace through the last quarter of the eighteenth century, and up to the 1840s. Writing from the perspective of the mid twentieth century, E.P. Thompson (1963) made plain his view of their impact on the rural working class:

> In village after village , enclosure destroyed the 'scratch-as-scratch-can' subsistence economy of the poor. The cottager without legal proof of rights was rarely compensated. The cotter who was able to establish his claim was left with a parcel of land inadequate for subsistence and a disproportionate share of the very high enclosure cost.

> Enclosure ... was a plain enough class robbery, played according to the rules of property and law laid down by a parliament of property-owners and lawyers.

But that invective is perhaps most relevant where the enclosure was of the common fields that had allocated land for raising crops close to the nucleated villages of the English lowlands. In the Colne Valley there is only one large area of parliamentary enclosure, the Golcar Enclosure, and that was of what would previously have been largely rough grazing on the edge of the moor, meeting the conditions described by Rennie et al. There was a second nearby parliamentary enclosure at Scammonden, along and beyond the northern watershed of the Valley.

The Golcar Enclosure was relatively late, 1823. It was surveyed by W.M. Pilkington of Thorne, York, and Fredk Jones of Milnsbridge, and will have followed a process described by Arthur Raistrick (1946) in his *Story of the Pennine Walls*:

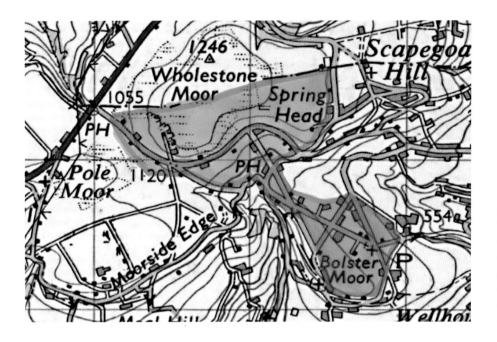

FIG. 17.
The area covered by the Golcar Enclosure. The enclosure covered the grazing below Wholestone Moor, known at the time as Hartshole Moor, and Bolster Moor below it.

Enclosures process

- a third of current landowners were required for a petition to be submitted to Parliament for a bill
- after the bill's 2nd reading, it goes to committee where petitions against the bill are heard. The committees were largely made up of other landowners – so there was (at least the perception of) systemic bias
- the 3rd reading and consideration by the Lords followed, and then Royal Assent
- post 1774 all petitions were required to be fixed to church doors for three Sundays in August and September
- normally three Commissioners were then appointed – mainly lawyers and agents
- the legislation imposed a duty to enclose within a specified period on those allocated plots – and there was then a duty to maintain the enclosure walls and tracks.

Whyte (2003) shows that enclosures were often followed quickly by sales of land as ownerships were consolidated, and often too by the building of new farmsteads. Both seem to have been the case for the Golcar enclosure. The Golcar Tythe map of 1849 shows that ownership of many of the allocated strips was quickly consolidated into fewer hands. At what became New Ing Farm, for instance, there were three owners established by the enclosure, John Blackburn, James Eastwood junior, and Joseph Lockwood. By 1849 all three holdings were owned by Samuel Walker, a clothier living at Westwood, and the field boundaries had been adjusted to their present form. The consolidated property was let to a family called Beaumont, who were listed in the 1841 and 1851 censuses as weavers and 'manufacturers' – presumably of cloth. The land use was reported as a mixture of meadow and arable – the latter probably oats. The current buildings, a terrace of two weavers' houses (then occupied by two generations of Beaumonts), with a barn attached and a single story dyehouse at the rear, were all in place.

Enclosure walls, whether the results of nineteenth century Acts of Parliament or late-eighteenth century enclosures of rough grazing and consolidations of small fields organised by the estate owners, were carried out by professional walling teams. Raistrick tells us that a good waller would complete seven yards a day, consuming approximately three tons of quarried stone as he did so. He describes walling teams, often made up of ex-miners, living in old barns, building from spring to autumn, and quarrying their own stone. They were apparently 'silent types'.

FIG. 18.
Enclosure Act landscape at Bolster Moor. Note the farmsteads built after the enclosure and in line with the new grid.

He quotes a typical specification for the walls, taken from the 1788 Grassington Act:
- good walls to be constructed within 12 months
- they should be 34" at their base
- they should be 6' high
- they should have coping stones of at least 4" thickness
- there should be 21 throughs per rood.
- the wall should be 16" broad beneath the coping stones
        … and that is how they remain in the current landscape.

———————

It is the pattern of the fields and the nature of walls that provides the fullest record from which one can discern the evolution of the landscape of the Colne Valley.

It is a highly legible record. As you travel along the hillsides you walk along tracks and lanes that are always bounded by walls. Sometimes you are on a double walled 'gate' taking you up to the moors. Sometimes you are walking along the head wall above an early landscape.

The more you observe the fields and walls the more you become conscious of their relationship to the history of the Valley. It is a longer one than is perhaps first appreciated, from the vaccary walls in the Wessenden Valley to the Golcar Enclosure of 1823, and it offers a clear testament to the evolution of the Valley's economy and settlement pattern.

FIG. 19.
Parliamentary enclosure wall, Meeting House Lane, Bolster Moor.

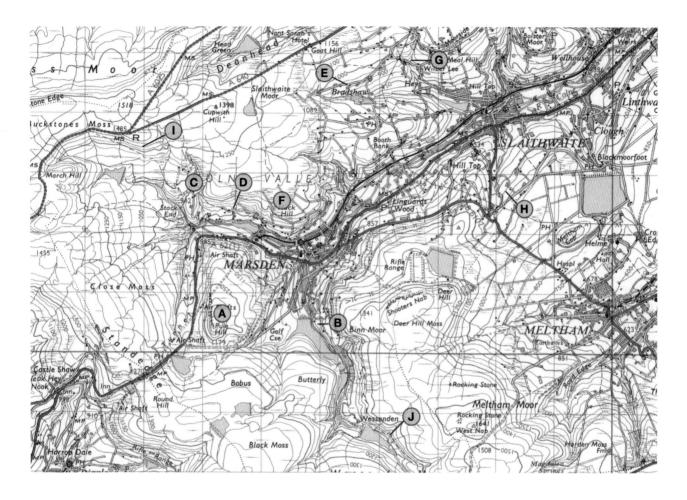

FIG. 20.

Field patterns and walls: locations

The letters follow the order in which the features are referred to in the text

A   *Pule Hill*
B   *Remains of Wessenden vaccary*
C   *Owlers*
D   *Walled track below Great Edge*
E   *Orthostats in wall on Bradshaw Lane*
F   *Stone Folds*
G   *Pinfold at Ainley Place*
H   *Hey Farm assart*
J   *Sheepfold in Wessenden Valley*

QUARRIES
AND DELPHS

IF THE FIELD patterns and walls of the Colne Valley hold its form and set its essential character, it is its quarries and delphs, the sources of the vast quantities of stone from which the walls were built, that add dramatic punctuation to the landscape.

There are more than eighty 'sandstone quarries' marked on the 1854 first edition OS map of the Colne Valley. Almost none are now worked, but they remain strong visual features. As with the field pattern, there is a chronology, and a story of settlement and economic development, to be read from what remains visible in the Valley.

Early stone sources – 'Lazyman delphs'

The earliest assart walls were made from found stones, cleared from the fields they enclosed. But as the pattern of fields extended along the valley sides,

FIG. 21.
This quarry face and roadway is at Worlow, on Pule Hill.

from the sixteenth century onwards, and particularly in the eighteenth and nineteenth centuries, more supplies were required. Wallers were expected to find their own materials, and very sensibly they opened up delphs, small quarries, as close as possible to their project. These were known as 'Lazyman delphs' – hardly fair, walling is hard, if absorbing and satisfying, work.

Delphs were opened up all over the hillsides, but most have long since disappeared back under the turf, leaving just a shallow depression in the ground.

Sustained quarry sites

Where the millstone grit forms outcrops, often towards the upper third of the valley sides, there are many much more substantial workings. These are where quarrying continued sporadically as demand recurred over many decades. The quarries are now long abandoned, but remain strong features in the landscape. They are explored by each generation of Valley children, and they are home to kestrels, pigeons, and the occasional peregrine falcon. They were worked for walling stone (known as 'dimensional stone'), flags, and thick Yorkshire roofing slates, all of which were dressed and prepared, or in the local dialect 'fettled', on site before being taken away down well engineered roadways and inclined planes. At some quarries the remains of the dressing sheds can still be found.

Pule Hill workings

Quarrying boomed with the developments of the nineteenth century: enclosures, mills, houses, canal, railway and reservoirs all demanded ample supplies of dressed stone. There were 120 quarries active in the Halifax and

FIG. 22.
Abandoned quarry workings under the edge of Wholestone Moor. There are still heaps of half-worked stone on the floor of the quarry (SE 0778 161).

FIG. 23.
Dressing shed below quarries on the South slope of Worts Hill (SE 0628 1563).

Huddersfield area in 1898 (Johnson, 2016). Some quarries, those at the most accessible faces of the Namurian Carboniferous Sandstone ledges that outcrop towards the tops of the valley sides, developed as long term, and large scale, commercial concerns serving far more than local demand. The 'Yorkstone' of Elland, Halifax and Huddersfield was paving London.

The most impressive group of workings in the Colne Valley are along the edges of Pule Hill, where they provide a dramatic gateway as you come over the Standedge watershed and begin to drop down through the top of the Valley towards Marsden.

There were five large quarries along the flanks of the hill during the peak years of the development of the Valley's economy, from the 1850s until the first decades of the twentieth century. All are shown on the 1854 6" OS map, and are listed in David Johnson's (2016) *Quarrying in the Yorkshire Pennines*:

- Netherley Quarry – shown as an 'old quarry' in 1892
- Nab End Quarry – owned by James Wood of Owlers from 1917 to 1930s
- Pinglet Head Quarry
- Worlow Quarry – still working in 1933
- Pule Edge Quarry – at the top of the inclined plane that rises from the A62. It produced paving setts.

During this period quarrying was a significant part of the local economy. The West Yorkshire Geological Trust's work on the *Rocks and Landscapes of Marsden* (Tymon, 2013) shows that two local families in particular, the Woods and the Whiteheads, were successful quarrymen and stone suppliers.

FIG. 24.
Dog holes in the surfaces of large stone blocks used to line the lock below Tunnel End .

They will have employed significant workforces, engaged in a range of tasks. David Johnson (2016) identifies:

- nicking – cutting the starter nicks, for use in splitting along beds
- the use of plugs and feathers – for cutting stone along beds
- creating a 'bottom deliver' – cutting below the face to produce a fall
- baring – fracturing and removing stone, to expose the beds of high quality stone for more careful working
- feighing and ridding – removing the overburden
- breaking and filling – breaking down large pieces of rock after an explosion
- the use of 'poppers' – pneumatic (later hydraulic) tools to break up rock
- broaching – using axes to clean up stone surfaces
- flag-fettling – the final tidying up of flagstones

Larger stones were moved by derricks, eventually steam driven, which used 'dogs' and chains to grip their loads. The dogs locked into notches (dog holes) cut into the faces of the blocks, and the mechanics of the pivots where the chains held the dogs ensured that the weight of the load tightened the grip. You can sometimes see dog holes in large stones incorporated into substantial structures. There are some under the railway bridge across John William Street in Huddersfield, and some on the side of the last canal lock before Tunnel End at Marsden.

Rocking Stone Quarry

There remains one sandstone quarry in the Valley, at Rocking Stone, which is still occasionally worked. It is invisible from the valley below, and is thus a dramatic surprise when it opens suddenly beneath your feet as you walk along the crest of Wholestone Moor. It is owned by Johnsons Wellfield who operate the large quarries at Crosland Hill, still a major national supplier of high quality building stone. At the time of writing it is dormant, but has recently been in use. Large blocks of stone were being taken by low-loader to the main Johnsons site for sawing into the dimensioned blocks and flags.

Ganister quarries

Not all quarries in the Valley produced building stone. Those along Shooters Nab, under Deer Hill Moss which forms the watershed between Marsden and Meltham, were worked for ganister, a particularly hard and fine grained sandstone, high in quartz content. They supplied the Meltham Silica Firebrick Company, which produced furnace linings and operated into the 1960s.

FIG. 25.
Rocking Stone Quarry. Briefly famous as the site used to film the TV series Jericho (SE 0764 1639).

FIG. 26.
Ganister quarry workings, forming a dramatic backdrop to Deer Hill Reservoir.

FIG. 27.
*Field below Badger Gate
(SE 0695, 1260).*

FIG. 28.
*Coal workings? Near to Coal
Gate, at the edge of Blake
Clough (SE 0478 1387).*

Coal in the Valley

There is little in the Valley's current landscape that indicates a history of coal extraction – but there was some. The 1854 OS 1st edition map shows coal pits below Shooters Nab, and at Lingards Wood Moor nearby. A little further down the same side of the valley is a rather oddly marked field (fig. 27). The pock marks might be the remains of bell pits, a medieval mining technique.

There is also a 'Coal Gate': the lane which runs along the other side of the valley from the hamlet of Bradshaw to the edge of Blake Clough. Close by is a stone hut amidst old workings, perhaps coal extraction, although nothing is marked on the OS map.

———

Quarries and delphs are the scars left on the Colne Valley landscape as its man-made features were constructed. Like other scars, they are strong visual markers – and they are important to the landscape as a whole. The quarry workings and inclined planes around Pule Hill and Shooters Nab add drama and a degree of grandeur above the expanses of moorland at the head of the valley. Smaller, older, workings are to be found on every hillside, where they have the effect of tying the neighbouring walls and buildings back to the land from which they were made.

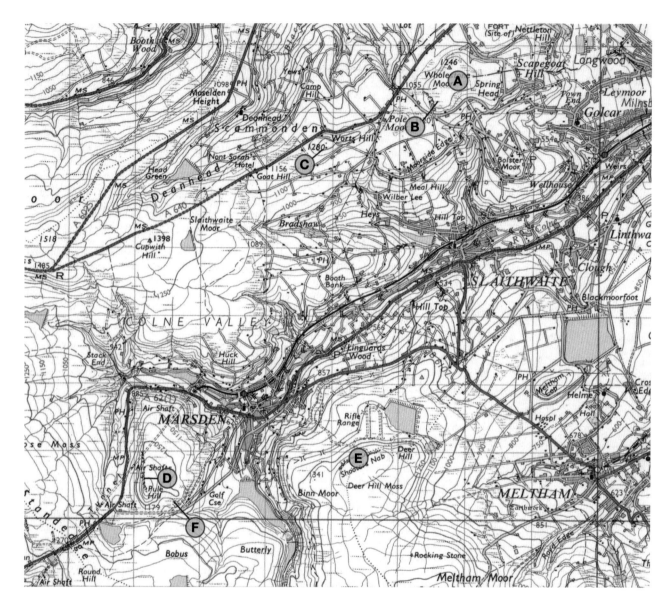

FIG. 29.

Quarries and Delphs: locations

A   *Wholestone Moor*
B   *Rocking Stones Quarry*
C   *Dressing sheds at Worts Hill*
D   *Pule Edge Quarry*
E   *Ganister quarries at Shooters Nab*
F   *Worlow Quarry*

THE SETTLEMENT PATTERN AND THE DUAL ECONOMY

TO DANIEL DEFOE the Pennines were 'the Andes of the North'. As he travelled over them from Lancashire in 1724 he recorded that:

> … we found the houses thicker and the villages greater in every bottom: the side of the hills which were very steep every way, were spread with houses, and that very thick: for the land being divided into small enclosures from two acres to seven acres each, seldom more: every three or four pieces of land had a house belonging to it.

> Then it was I began to perceive the reason and nature of the thing, and found that this division of the land into small pieces, and scattering of the dwellings was done for the convenience of the business which the people were generally employed in …. this business is the clothing trade…

> We could see that almost at every house there was a tenter and almost on every tenter a piece of cloth, or kersie, or shalloon … As our road passed among them, wherever we passed any house we found a rill or gutter of running water … and at every considerable house was a manufacture or workhouse.

> Then, as every clothier must keep a horse, perhaps two to fetch and carry for the use of his manufacture; … so every manufacturer generally keeps a cow or two, or more, for his family and this employs the two, or three, or four pieces of enclosed land about his house, for they scarce sow corn enough for their cocks and hens.

He was traversing from Littleborough to Halifax, and thus a few miles further North, but he described a pattern that remains a distinctive feature of the Colne Valley hillsides. In the same passage he also recognised other enduring strengths of South Pennines life:

The store of good ale which flows plentifully in the most mountainous part of this country, seems abundantly to make up for all the inclemencies of the season.

Earliest settlements

It is the stone-built houses and barns that began to replace earlier wooden booths and shelters from the late medieval period onwards that are evident in the current landscape.

There are very few houses that are early by national standards. The hamlet at Slaithwaite Hall, once a seat of the Tyas family, incorporates a single storey building that Philip Ahier (1933) identified as being fourteenth century. The current buildings are thought to contain remnants of the hall itself. Across the valley, Linthwaite Hall, which still stands, is thought to date from the fifteenth century.

There may be others: what was once the Launds Inn, above Clough Head, apparently dates from the fourteenth century. Robert Broadbent, whose family ran that and many other inns in the area, has traced land tax payments for Launds earlier still, into the thirteenth century (see at *www.laundsinnmuseum.co.uk*). There are other old buildings in the valley bottom (the Manor House in Slaithwaite has a sixteenth century origin) but no other substantial early houses on the hillsides.

FIG. 30.

The hamlet of Slaithwaite Hall

FIG. 31.
Linthwaite Hall

The most immediate contrast is with Upper Calder Valley where fine sixteenth and seventeenth century yeomen's houses are found in many hamlets, perhaps because the broader valley sustained rather wealthier farming. Perhaps also because of the different histories of land tenure. There seem to have been few wealthy yeomen in the Colne Valley, and the landowning gentry generally lived elsewhere.

Medieval settlement pattern

The Slaithwaite Manor Court rolls tell us where the settlements were in the mid-sixteenth and seven-teenth centuries and probably reflect the extent of the medieval settlement pattern. Those attending the Court meetings came from *(the entries for each meeting show only names that appear for the first time)*:

1543   New Hey, Warenbotham, Rocher, Shaghkarr, Bothebank, Slaghtwate Hall, Rughey, Shaghfelde

1544   Northende, Hall, Launds, Slaghthwaite, Badgeryate, Lyngarthes

1546   Paroke (means Small Enclousre – see Smith, 1963), Bothe, Wilborelee, Birkes, Netherende, Thorngapp, Wolrode, Wollerodegrene, Cupwith Dyke

1548   Shayfield

1549   Moregate, Morecote, Carr Inge (Carr means marsh – Smith, 1963), Newhouse

1551   Faldingworth Hey

1560   Morehey, Birkynhey

1570   Chapell, Golker Common
1593   Blackstones, Waterside, Highfield, Castell, The Hey, Barntts, Slode
        (Slippery Place? – Smith, 1963), Bentts, Stoneybutt, Call Bottom
1635   Rotcher, Anleyplace, Lathe, Copp, Shawfield, Mealehill, Parkeygate,
        Halme, Holt, Malenfield, Pighell, Townfield, Enghead, Heyend,
        Crimble land (Crimble = small plot of land – Smith, 1963),
        Milnreield, Milneholme
1638   Raw, Playnes, Broadcarr, Bradshawe, Westgate, Bryan Place,
        Whiteroydhead, Bridgend

A substantial number of these place names are still used in the Valley today. They are plotted in fig. 32. What emerges echoes the early development of the Colne Valley field pattern. The places mentioned are concentrated on the shoulders of the valley, where by the fifteenth century the earlier assarts had become the nuclei of larger hamlets. The geology, of water-holding sandstone interleaved by bands of impervious mudstones and shales, gives rise to springs high on the hillsides, thus allowing dwellings with immediate access to water – one of the features that so impressed Defoe.

Those hamlets are there still: Wilberlee, Westwood, Bradshaw, Meal Hill, Castle, Launds, Ainley Place, Holme, Shawfield, Booth Bank, Cop Hill, Badger Gate. All stand just above steep slopes, where the land flattens a little before rising again to the high moors.

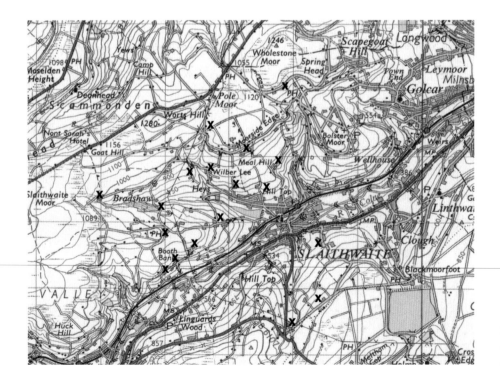

FIG. 32.
Place names that appear in the Manor Rolls.

FIG. 33.
New House, above Slaithwaite (SE 0718 1311).

FIG. 34.
Westwood Edge.

It is difficult to discern evidence of fifteenth or sixteenth century houses within these hamlets, but there are some that seem to be from the seventeenth century, for example at New House above Slaithwaite on the South side of the valley.

Further along the same hillside are houses with eighteenth century date stones. Further up the valley still, at Green Top, Old Mount Road, Marsden, there is a surviving seventeenth century date stone, of 1671, and the date of 1611 is inscribed on a lintel.

FIG. 35.
Date stone on Nathans farmstead below Badger Hey (SE 0664 1261).

FIG. 36.
Date stone at Stubbing, Marsden (SE 0572 1233).

FIG. 37.
Date stone at Hill Top, Slaithwaite - once the home of Robert Meeke (SE 0801 1430).

FIG. 38.
Date stone at Holt Head (SE 0803 1246).

The dual economy and a non-nucleated landscape

The landscape Daniel Defoe describes evolved in the seventeenth and eighteenth centuries. The economy of the Valley was then balanced on the two strong legs of making woollen cloth lengths and farming. On the whole, it seems to have been a strong economy that afforded a reasonable standard of living. W.B. Crump (1938) quotes Watson's *Farming Notes* of 1775:

> There is scarcely a single instance in the whole parish of a man's living entirely by farming: the land therefore is divided into small parcels, everyone who can, taking just as much as will yield a sufficient quantity of milking butter for the support of his family; on this account it proves difficult for many of the poor to get these things, which is the only considerable disadvantage they labour under, and which is by much over-balanced by a constant supply of work, good wages, and plenty of most necessaries of life, so I know not any country where upon the whole they live better.

It is the relationship between the two economies that formed the characteristic distribution of stone dwellings along the hillsides and which, with the reticule of the walled fields, has set the distinctive form of the Colne Valley landscape (See fig. 46 on p.47 which shows this pattern clearly).

The economies developed together, but each has had its own history as the landscape, technology, and patterns of trade have evolved.

The early development of the woollen cloth trade

According to Heaton (1965), woollen cloth production first progressed from meeting purely local demand to becoming a nascent exporting industry in the fourteenth century. As the production and trade became more important they became increasingly regulated. An Act of Parliament in 1376 ensured that any exported cloth was properly finished by fulling (the process of scouring away any fatty residues and washing the woven cloth). By 1450 further legislation protected the trade by banning the import of woollen goods and the export of raw wool. Nationally the number of cloth pieces exported to Europe went from 5000 in 1350 to 84,000 in 1509. Another Act of 1563 defined a regulated structure of masters, journeymen, and apprenticeships. The courts record various cases enforcing the requirement that a webster, weaver, or mercer must have served an apprenticeship. In 1604 minimum and maximum wages were established (although Heaton reports that this legislation was largely ignored).

Cloth piece sizes were defined, and policed, from the Magna Carta onwards, as, 'Una latitudo pannorum tinctorum et russettorum et habergettorum, scilicet duae ulnae infra listas' which set the width of a piece, whether russet

FIG. 39.
Tenter posts at Warehouse Hill, Marsden. Numerous arrays of tenter posts are marked on the OS 1st edition, including several sets just above Town End at Golcar and on Golcar Flats, but these in Marsden are the only local survivors (SE 0509 1177).

or otherwise dyed, at two lengths of the lower arm (i.e. 'duae ulnae' – two ulna bones). By the late medieval period this standard was enforced through the 'Ulnage' laws, with a fee taxed at 1d per piece for the attachment of ulnage seals.

There were disputes over the impact of tentering – the stretching of drying cloths between tenter posts – on ulnage. In 1597 there was an attempt to outlaw the process of tentering. The legal to and fro that followed was only finally resolved when the practice was protected as a legal procedure by an Act of 1623.

Tensions increased over the rate of the Ulnage tax in the late 1630s, after a period of decline in the trade. There were street fights and also court action. In their defence of the latter the Yorkshire clothiers prayed in aid the strengths of their community, and emphasised that there are was no Popery in their parishes:

> By the special grace of God, their is not one Popish Recusant inhabiting in the great and populous parish [of Halifax]

They also made the Yorkshireman's claim, to a London audience, that:

> … the places which [the clothiers] inhabitt being soe mountainous and rough, soe barren and unfruitful as it will not suffice to yield victualls for the third part of the inhabitants, and the poor that spin the wooll there, though they work very harde, cannot gaine for theire labour fowre pence a day towards their livinge.

They won their case.

In his history of the Yorkshire woollen and worsted industries, Heaton reports many references to cloth-makers in the Wakefield manorial rolls of the thirteenth century. But nationally the Yorkshire production was not dominant; it was more than matched in the South and East – in Gloucestershire, Somerset, Wiltshire and Suffolk. Even so, by the late sixteenth century the area around Halifax had become relatively wealthy on the trade. It largely used wool imported from elsewhere – the breeds of sheep that thrived on the Pennines yielded coarse wool, only suitable for weaving rough cloth.

Cloth making in the Colne Valley

The trade seems to have developed later in the Colne Valley than in the Calder Valley, but in their *History of the Huddersfield Woollen Industry*, Crump and Ghorbal (1935) record evidence from a trade register of 1533 of local cloth makers who were by then well-established. It lists:

Richard More of Owtlayn   Thomas Campynott of Slatwayt
John Bamfforth of Crymble   John Walker of Westwood
Robert Walker of Golcar

Producing a cloth piece requires a complex sequence of operations, which typically engaged the whole family. The patriarchal structure was evident:
- the father bought the wool,
- the wife and children carded and spun it,
- the father, and possibly a journeyman, dyed, spun and wove the piece,
- it was taken to fulling mill,
- and then to a stall in the cloth hall.

The clothier's family would finish an average of two pieces of kersey (a length of cloth) a week. They would also have a small holding of perhaps three acres where they would keep a cow, a pig, and some poultry – and perhaps a horse, although many carried the pieces on their backs.

As the economy developed the trades became more specialised and were carried out by a network of workers, organised by the clothier – often the weaver. By the time, in the mid-nineteenth century, that the domestic industry was giving way to mass production in the valley-bottom mills, it was reported that the production of four dozen broad cloths, each 12 yds by 1.75 yds, required 60 workers:
- 12 persons dressing and dyeing
- 30 spinning and carding
- 12 weaving and shearing
- 6 odd jobs and taking wool to fuller, etc

The cloth market and international trade

By the seventeenth century Yorkshire clothiers were travelling to London for the annual St Bartholomew fair – to sell kerseys and dozens (another type of cloth piece). Later there was a continuous market through Blackwell Hall, on Basinghall Street. It included a Northern Hall, dealing with 5000 pieces by 1622. A 1638 court case refers to annual Yorkshire production of 80,000 kerseys, of which 60,000 were exported, largely through Hull.

The earliest local cloth market was in Almondbury, which was thriving from the thirteenth century onwards. A Huddersfield cloth market developed in the seventeenth century, and a cloth hall was built by Sir John Ramsden in 1766.

The Cloth Hall was described in Pigot's Trade Directory of 1834:

It is a large circular edifice, two stories high, divided, on the one side, into separate compartments, or shops, and on the other, into open stalls, for the accommodation of the country manufacturers of woollen cloths. There are also two central avenues of stalls, for the same purpose, and the number of manufacturers now attending there

FIG. 40.
Huddersfield Cloth Hall.

on the market day (Tuesday) is about 600. If to this be added, the great number (particularly in the fancy line) who have ware-rooms in various parts of the town, some estimate may be formed of the immense extent of business transacted weekly in Huddersfield. The doors are opened early in the morning of the marketday, and closed at half-past twelve o'clock at noon, they are again opened at three in the afternoon, for the removal of cloth &c.

It was pulled down in the 1930s, apparently disturbing a large community of rats, and the site, having been home for the town's ABC cinema for many years, is now occupied by Sainsbury's and Specsavers. The entrance, with its cupola, was reerected in the grounds of the Tolson Museum, where it still stands.

The magnificent Halifax Piece Hall opened in 1779 and is recently restored. It is standing there, surrounded by its tiered arcades of trading rooms, that the scale, and the confidence, of the eighteenth and nineteenth century cloth trade comes most powerfully to life.

A clothier's trade

A picture of the scale and reach of the successful clothier's trading network emerges from the notebooks of Joseph Holroyd, a local cloth factor. His correspondence of late 1706 and early 1707 (Heaton, 1914) was with forty factors and other correspondents in Germany and Holland, just one of whom takes £17,000 worth of kerseys in 12 months (about £4m worth at 2020 values). Holroyd took a 1.5 percent commission on his sales.

But the trade had its risks. In the two years covered one shipment is lost at sea and another is captured by the French. In September 1706 he writes in pursuit of the stock lost in the shipwreck:

> Sir
>
> I have letter from mr John Field of Hull that ye package No D was shipt on board Tho Wright. Said ship was lost ye 25 past near Yarmouth which I am sorry for all suferers. Mr Major Wilson of Leeds who pkt the same and others that is in the ship hath sent a man to Yarmouth to the care of all goods he pack't. I desire yow wold to him at Yarmouth at ye post office ... how yow old have him order your packe. Thmas Wright master had 25 cloth pa on board and we heare 17 of them cast ashore I hope yours will be one of them which I shall be glad to heare.

Holroyd was operating at the top of the trading pyramid. For the individual weaver work was hard and rewards modest. But there were satisfactions, and some balance, in the work whilst it was rooted in the domestic economy. Certainly there were regrets for those who moved into the industrial weaving sheds of the valley bottoms during the latter part of the nineteenth century. This is taken from the autobiography of William Heaton, *An Old Soldier and a Wandering Lover* [!], written in 1857:

> I [...] worked in a small chamber, overlooking Luddenden Churchyard. I used to get out in the fields and woods around the village at meal-times, and listen to the songs of the summer birds, or watch the trembling waters of the Luddon, as they murmured melodiously over the pebbly brook. I have watched the butterfly dance on the lovely flowers, and heard with rapture the hum of the wold bee in the foxglove.

But towards the end of his life he is working at Crossley's carpet mills in Halifax:

> I frequently wish now for my churchyard cot, and my busy loom, that I could walk in the fields at the close of day and at my leisure hours. But it is all over; I must continue to work amidst the clatter of machinery.

The farming economy

The modern landscape of the valley hillsides is almost entirely pastoral. The fields receive various levels of attention: some are regularly ploughed and reseeded; some are fertilised each year, most often with muck from cattle sheds; most are cut for hay and then silage each summer – some are slowly reverting to rough grazing and rushes. They support some cattle: a dairy herd, and some bullocks for fattening during the summer months. There are sheep, mostly Texels or hobby herds of rarer breeds, on some fields throughout the year. Horses are common, and there are currently some exotic herds of alpacas. (Perhaps they take comfort from Defoe's comparison of the Pennines to the Andes.)

Farms in the Valley have always been small. In 1846 80 percent of those in Slaithwaite and Lingards parish were of less than ten acres. They were run as family concerns, mostly without hired labour.

Crops

Land use was more diverse when the dual economy was at its height. The form of the laithes (barns), with their threshing floors between opposing barn doors, implies some grain crops, as is to be expected where families would have been concerned to feed themselves and their beasts. The crop returns of 1801 show that the grain was almost entirely oats – a crop that can be productive even on poor land (Thomson and Turner, 1978). There were 185.5 acres given over to oat production in Linthwaite parish, in contrast to a total of 15 acres for wheat, barley, potatoes and turnips combined.

The proportion of land used for crops increased during the Napoleonic wars, and during the first and second world wars. Even in the 1960's Joshua Roper used to visit local farms with a steam threshing engine. But the soil is essentially poor, and the areas flat enough to plough efficiently are limited. The Valley is best adapted to pastoral use.

Pastures and rough grazing

There have long been sheep here, especially Lonks, a breed adapted to the rather tough conditions of the South Pennines, and then Texels. But it would be wrong to assume that the strengths of the wool trade implied that they dominated the landscape. The weavers always brought in raw wool, originally from elsewhere in the UK, later from northern Germany and Silesia, and then from New Zealand and Australia.

It was rather the raising of cattle that dominated from the medieval vaccaries onwards, and which did most to shape the landscape. The early fields on the valley sides sit below larger enclosures below the moors, on land taken in from rough grazing during the seventeenth to nineteenth centuries, with or without an Enclosure Act. The rough grazing was stinted, so that each small farm had a right to graze a set number of beasts. Access was via the walled 'gates', described earlier, which prevented the beasts trespassing on the land of others as they were moved up for the summer months.

The sixteenth and seventeenth century Manorial Rolls are peppered with the adjudication of offences related to the keeping of stock. Individuals are fined for keeping unyoked swine and for allowing their cattle to stray. They are exhorted to make up their fences, to use particular tracks when moving their beasts, and to maintain gates (or 'yates') by their holdings.

Other misdemeanours include recovering beasts from the pinfold by force, hare coursing in times of snow, eating geese or pigs on the Lord's day – and harbouring 'rogues and vagabonds'.

Cloth making and farming combined in the dual economy

Jennings et al. (1992) found evidence that 34 out of 47 farmers in their Calder Valley study area in the seventeenth century were also textile workers. The work of the Marsden History Group on probate wills and inventories (Seidel, 2013) provides evidence of a similar dual economy in the Colne Valley. The balance of working lives, integrating the making of woollen cloth pieces and small-scale farming, comes to life in the narratives left by two individuals.

Cornelius Ashworth (1782 – 1816)

In his autobiography, Cornelius Ashworth, a weaver and hill farmer from the Calder Valley, gives a graphic account of that dual economy in the late eighteenth and early nineteenth centuries. (Davis, Petford and Senior, 2011).

He owned 16 acres where he and his family raised cows and grew oats. They had rights on the unenclosed common at Ovenden Moor, above Halifax. He describes the use of a midden and the routine of fertilising the fields each March, and the cutting of channels to irrigate the fields and encourage grass growth. Hay making, each July, was carried out by a gang of itinerant mowers. The cattle were turned out on to the cut fields, to feed off the 'eddish' (the stubble) and then brought in from October to April. The oats were harvested in September and threshed and winnowed in October. His rights on the moor were extinguished by an Enclosure Act of 1814. He received one acre and two roods of the enclosed land, and had to meet costs amounting to £6 2s 10d.

Weaving was largely his winter occupation – every day from October to February. He produced half a piece a week, 30 yards of worsted cloth, and carried the finished pieces to a cloth agent. He used niches in the field walls to set runs of sticks, for 'warping', or sorting, yarn and for 'tentering', or stretching, the finished cloth. In addition he supplemented his weaving income with walling, building and, rather surprisingly, dealing in hops.

The breadth of Cornelius Ashworth's activities was impressive. He was also an active evangelist and evidently a disputatious Non-Conformist.

Benjamin Wilson

Writing some 60 years later, Benjamin Wilson (whose autobiography was published in 1887) described his early life as a farm and textile worker. He would rise before five in the morning and walk with a donkey to a farm, where he would milk the cows before delivering milk to the neighbouring mill terraces. In the afternoon he would set card teeth for the machines used to prepare fleeces for spinning – 1500 teeth for a half-penny. His average income was nine shillings (45 pence) a week.

He too had a range of trades. At different times, sometimes overlapping, he worked as a weaver, a comber, a navvy on railway construction, a barer of stone in the delph (unskilled work at a quarry). He was an active Chartist, and a member of the early local co-operative society – and a member of the temperance movement (Burnett, Vincent, and Mayall, 1984).

Industrialisation of the valley bottom, the decline of domestic cloth production and new markets for farm produce

Benjamin Wilson lived on to the late 1860s, and thus saw the surge of industrialisation in the valley bottom of the second half of the nineteenth century.

Large mills came late to the Earl of Dartmouth's Slaithwaite estate. Milner Tomlinson's research, *Landlord Promotion of Agrarian Improvement in a Pennine Valley 1843–1853*, tells the story of the Fourth Earl's attempts to maintain the social structure he had inherited – of tenant farmers who lived and worked in a stable social order overseen by the land owner, his agent, and the parson. But the order was under threat as the market for handloom production was driven down, first by the disruptions to trade caused by early nineteenth century wars in Europe, and then by the overwhelming competition of the more efficient production in the new industrial textile mills. The living standards of his tenants declined sharply.

The Earl sought means to sustain his tenants. In the 1840s a number of large landowners became engaged in the 'Spade Husbandry and Stall Feeding' movement, as a means of increasing crop yields and improving the lives of their tenants. Lord Dartmouth, along with Frederick Thynne, his agent, and Rev C A Hulbert, the vicar of Slaithwaite, promoted a Spade Husbandry association on the estate from 1843 to 1854.

The Earl funded courses in husbandry, a library of techniques, the provision of tools – and an annual competition for small-holding produce. He also created five model farms where spade husbandry could be demonstrated in contrasting circumstances – on either side of the valley, and at different altitudes.

At Barrett Clough land was allocated for a range of crops:

- Cabbages 5 acres
- Carrots 5.5 acres
- Oats 1.75 acres
- Vetches 1 acre
- Potatoes 5 acres
- Turnips 0.25 acres
- Grass for hay 2.5 acres

The Earl also pursued schemes that gave work to needy tenants whilst improving his estate. Varley Road – the 'New Line' as it was known – was driven from Slaithwaite up the South side of the valley to Holt Head, to join the turnpike which linked Huddersfield and Meltham to Marsden. Slaithwaite Moor was improved and opened up by the Crimea Causeways that now box off the Pole Moor radio masts.

FIG. 41.
The Crimea Causeways – straight tracks between fields on the Moorside plateau, drained by a scheme funded by the Earl of Dartmouth in the 1840s (Ordnance Survey, Colne Valley First edition 6").

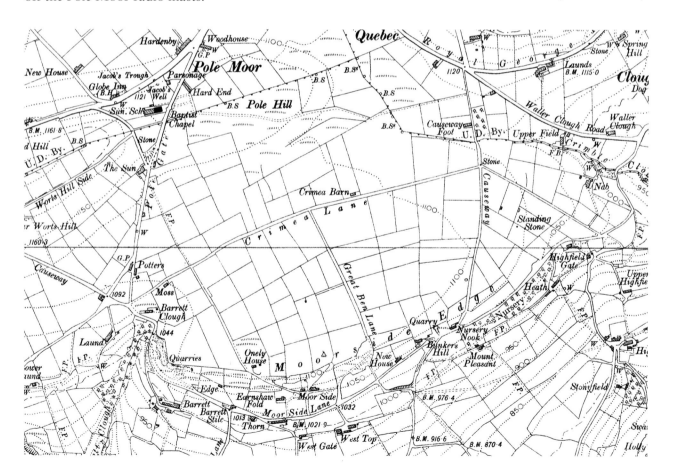

It was a paternalistic response to circumstances summarised by the Earl's agent, Thynne, in his 1846 report to the tenants:

Handloom weavers find it difficult to obtain any employment and almost impossible to obtain constant employment and the wages are so reduced that a bare living is best afforded. (Tomlinson)

Arguably it was also an attempt to sustain a dependent relationship between tenant and landowner on an estate under pressure from the new order created by entrepreneurs and mill workers. The Rev Hulbert was enthusiastic too about the beneficial impacts on morals and sobriety that he saw as flowing from the good, honest, hard labour of the spade work.

In any event, the movement could not hold back the tide of the industrial revolution from the estate for long. The railway through the Valley was opened in 1849 – and the fourth Earl died in 1853. His successor took a different approach. He changed the nature of landholdings on the estate so that the new entrepreneurs had the long term security, through freeholds or 999 year leases, that made it sensible to invest, and from the 1860s onwards Slaithwaite was transformed by the building of large mills.

The rapid growth of a population living in mill terraces made farming commercial in its own right for a while. Suddenly there were local households living away from the land and hungry for perishable foods that could not travel far, milk and eggs in particular. (See Benjamin Wilson's way of life, above.) This helped the valley-side economy adjust to the loss of domestic cloth production as that side of the dual economy died away.

FIG. 42.
Far Worts Hill Farm – still with a dairy herd, and still supplying the Valley (SE 0627 1555).

Briggs dairy farm is still in business, at Far Worts Hill. Egg production also remained strong until well after the Second World War. The owner of New Ing Farm raised White Wynotts in the 1960s, and battery sheds are still a common sight, although many are now either re-purposed or deteriorating. Those at the head of Crimble Clough were a going concern into the 2000s. Their owner was born on the property and had an extensive delivery round to small shops for his egg production, across the Pennines into the Lancashire mill towns as well as to local villages (Walker, 2018).

A Colne Valley vernacular

The dual economy of the South Pennines evolved its own vernacular architecture.

Many dwellings from the eighteenth and nineteenth centuries are versions of the laithe house form, characteristic of upland West Yorkshire. Brunskill (1971) describes their particular layout: a two storey dwelling, one room deep, with a central passageway – and a barn (a 'laithe') and a byre or 'mistal' for the beasts, often all in line and under the same roof, but entered through separate doorways. The barn would have high doors, often on opposite sides of a threshing floor, where the through breeze would enable the winnowing of the crop – a form that confirms the earlier significance of various grain crops in a landscape in which they are no longer to be found.

A particular feature of some of the Colne Valley laithe houses is their continuous runs of mullioned windows on the upper storey, facing South to gain the maximum amount of light for the close work of threading bobbins and operating looms. They are weavers' laithe houses, a particular form that evolved through the Valley's dual economy.

The pattern of weavers' houses, or short terraces, perhaps with a barn attached, each sitting within a small holding of three or four small fields but each within hailing distance (on a calm day) of its neighbour, and each with access to running water, still gives punctuation to the field pattern of the valley sides.

It has fixed the landscape partly because most large scale development in the twentieth and twenty-first centuries has been along the valley bottoms, and partly because it has proved a highly adaptable form. Although there are now few full time farmers in the Colne Valley, there are many local households who make good use of their small holdings. They raise sheep, fatten beef stock, or provide stabling – but they also have full-time jobs that sustain them and their families. They may be hauliers, or builders, teachers, health workers, entrepreneurs, bureaucrats. The settlement pattern continues to work well for them. Walls are (mostly) maintained. The eighteenth and nineteenth century houses are in good order.

FIG. 43.
Laithe house at Wool Royd, Laund Road, Slaithwaite (SE 0606 1474).

FIG. 44.
Laithe House at Slades, Heath Road, Linthwaite (SE 1053 1432).

FIG. 45.
Laithe House at Stubbing, Marsden (SE 0572 1233).

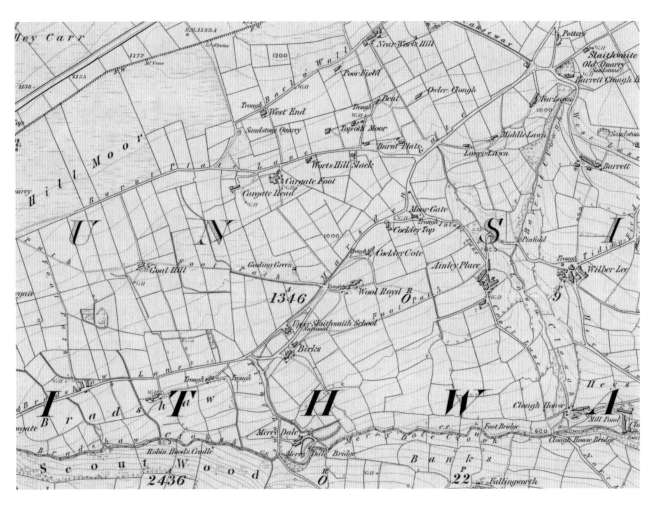

FIG. 46.
Section of the 1st edition Ordnance Survey 6" map of the Colne Valley, showing the distributed settlement pattern that evolved alongside the dual textile/farming economy.

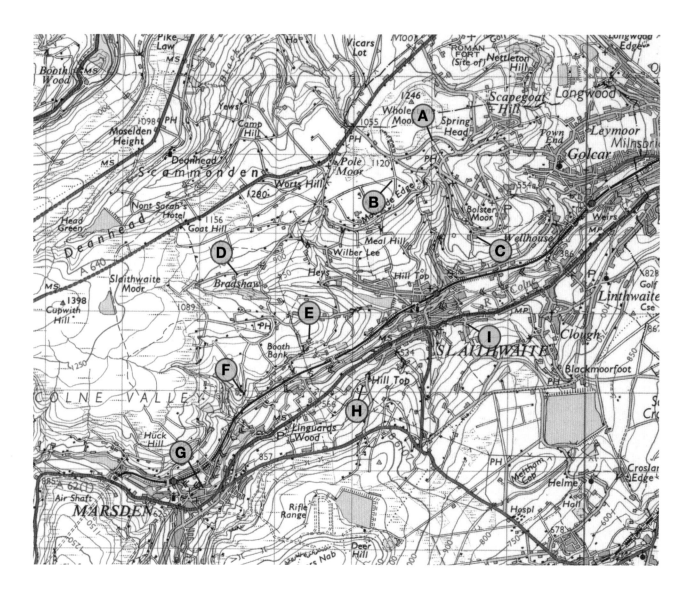

FIG. 47.

Settlement pattern: locations

A   Harts Hole
B   Crimea causeways
C   Westwood Edge
D   Bradshaw
E   Shawfields
F   Slaithwaite Hall
G   Tenter posts at Warehouse Hill
H   Newhouse
I   Linthwaite Hall

NON-CONFORMISM
– CHAPELS AND
SUNDAY SCHOOLS

AS YOU STOP to take in the landscape along the valley sides, among the walls, houses and farm buildings there will often be a chapel or a Sunday school in sight. If your view is expansive you may be able to pick out several.

They have a dignified presence, but not the emphatic tower or steeple that would signify one of the Anglican churches of the established order and its social hierarchy. These are mostly the buildings of the Non-Conformists – the groups whose approach to worship was based on dissenting religious doctrine. They are sturdy evidence of the collective confidence and assertion of communities whose self-reliance, trade connections, and increasing literacy had nurtured habits of independent thought and self-organisation.

The chapels provided a rhythmic, weekly, focus to the lives of the families engaged in the dual economy, across the dispersed settlement pattern of the hillsides.

The significance of the Sunday assembly at the chapel, the singing and making of music, the power of the sermon and the sense of being members

FIG. 48.

Sunnybank Baptist Chapel, a quiet presence amongst the short terraces of the Bolster Moor settlement.

of the saved elect, quite apart from the other churches and chapels: all are brought to life in *Ben O'Bills* the Luddite novel of D.F.E. Sykes (the Colne Valley historian) and G.H. Walker first published in 1898. Ben O'Bills and his family lived at Holme, the hamlet that lies half way up Cop Hill, above Slaithwaite. Each Sunday, each 'Lord's Day', they walked some two miles to Pole Moor, first dropping down into the bottom of Merrydale and then climbing steeply up through Wilberlee. As they neared the chapel:

> We could see the men quitting the burial ground and the little public house hard by, and all in their Sunday clothes, folk were coming from every part for the Sunday service, not hurrying, and with no air of business, but solemnly and seriously, talking little, and with thoughts, like their faces, set Zionwards.

Theirs was a community of Calvinist Baptists, led by the pastor Abraham Webster. The hymn singing was supported by a double bass, viol, and clarinet up in the loft. The sermon was powerful. It reinforced the sense that those who had assembled from their homes along the valley were a select community:

> ...oh! it was fine to hear little Parson Webster. How he rejoiced over the elect! How he lamented over the unregenerate! It was very comforting to hear, for we were the elect, the Erastians of the Church and the Arminians of the chapel in the valley we well understood to be those of outer darkness.

The Erastians were those who believed that the Church should be under the control of the state. The Arminians were also Baptists, but ones who did not share the Calvinists' belief in pre-destined salvation for the elect – i.e. the true members of the sect.

The roots of Non-Conformism in the Valley, and the opposition of the establishment

Dissent from the established, state, church became vigorous in England during the seventeenth century. It drew on the fifteenth and sixteenth century reformation in Europe, but also on the search for new frameworks for power and belief that accompanied the upheavals in the old order of the English Civil War. It was often repressed by the authorities, ruthlessly at times. It was not until the Glorious Revolution of 1688 and the Act of Toleration of 1689 that it became possible for dissenters to meet openly in their own places of worship.

Dissenting belief found fertile ground in the West Yorkshire Pennines and took root early. The Quaker Settlement at High Flatts, ten miles or so to the South of the Valley, was established in the 1650s (in a barn) and still meets.

By the nineteenth century the larger Quaker meeting house at Paddock, on the edge of the Valley, was operating, as it does to this day. The history of the Quakers of High Flatts, Wooldale and Midhope is set out in *Plain Country Friends* (Bower and Knight, 1987).

But it was Baptist congregations that made the earliest impact in the Colne Valley. A Scot, a potter called Michael Morton whose family were Presbyterian exiles who had settled in Salendine Nook, is thought to have led the first Baptist services in the Huddersfield area. Stock (1874) states that the Morton family arrived in the sixteenth century and opened a small chapel in the 1560s. By the late seventeenth century they were leading a Baptist community in services, discretely, in another barn, at Quarmby. The group was active when the Act of Toleration came into force and they could worship openly for the first time:

> ... The scene is an ancient barn. The doors open and two men come through, one is old, the other of middle age. The old man rises and the service begins as he reads Isiah Chapter 40 ... Comfort Ye My people ... The sermon has as its text 'Watchmen what of the night? The morning cometh' and the speaker recounts the difficulties under which his followers have laboured. At this point he shows them a piece of paper – their licence, and dwells on what this means. The blessed morning has come; the big barn doors are open for public worship and, please God, the open door shall never be taken away again.

It was this community that built the Salendine Nook Baptist Church in the 1740s.

The Chapel at Pole Moor was an offshoot, the first in the Colne Valley. It was built in the 1790s – in an isolated position on the lip of the valley, 1150 feet up and visible for miles around. The location tells its own story – this is

FIG. 49.

The Salendine Nook Baptist Community meeting before their chapel was built, taken from Stock (1874).

FIG. 50.
*Pole Moor Chapel -
standing like a strong
older sibling at the end
of an isolated terrace of
houses, high on the North
side of the valley.*

a chapel that could hardly be more remote from the established churches in Slaithwaite, Marsden, and Golcar. It was the meeting place of the Calvinist elect amongst the weavers, quarrymen, farmers and carters of the hillsides. It also lies just over the the boundary in Scammonden, beyond the control of the Dartmouth Estate.

The Earls of Dartmouth made strong common cause with the vicars of Slaithwaite to discourage the Non-Conformist congregations. Theirs was the old authority of squire and rector and they were not keen to see it weakened by free-thinking groups and radical preachers. The strength of the Luddite and Chartist causes in the first half of the nineteenth century would have intensified an opposition that was perhaps as much political as doctrinal – they were defending a social structure that was standing against a tide of change.

Milner Tomlinson's work on the estate and Church captures the work of the Fourth Earl and the vicar, Charles Hulbert, and Frederick Thynne, the Earl's agent, as they defended the old order through the middle of the nineteenth century. Their paternalistic responses to economic hardship have already been described but their sympathy for the estate's tenants did not extend to their religious beliefs. They stood firm against allowing the building of chapels on estate land. As a result the early Baptist chapels in the Valley were nearly all built beyond the estate's boundaries.

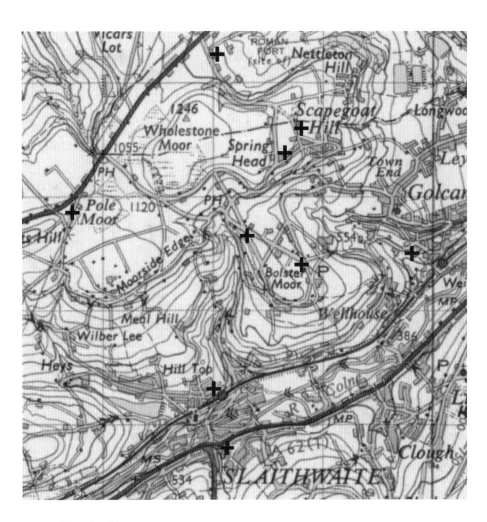

FIG. 51.

Distribution of Baptist Chapels in the Colne Valley.

Growth and schisms

The map (fig. 51) shows the nine Baptist chapels that stood in the Valley at the close of the nineteenth century, mostly on the hillsides of the southern flank of the valley, and none in either of the two parishes, either side of the river Colne, that make up Marsden.

The building of chapel after chapel reflected the increasing population of the Valley, which tripled from 7,600 to 25,200 in the nineteenth century, and the growth of Non-Conformism within that population. But, at least in the first third of the century, it also seems to have been driven by the doctrinal differences illustrated by the contempt for Erastians and Arminians felt by the congregation described in *Ben O'Bills*. During this period each new chapel represented a division within the Baptist movement as much as its overall expansion.

Even the formation of the Pole Moor Baptist community seems to have been as much the outcome of a falling out with the then Anglican curate at

Slaithwaite, Thomas Wilson, as a response to the strengthening appeal of Calvinism. *The Annals of the Church in Slaithwaite* (Hulbert, 1864) report that the curate antagonised a local family by adjudicating against them in a dispute over the ownership of eggs laid by hens that had strayed on to a neighbour's land. The family responded by breaking from his congregation and inviting a member of the Salendine Nook Baptist community to lead them in a new group. Whatever the truth of this origin story, the group clearly found a sustaining conviction. They met for some time in an upstairs room at the 'Silent Woman' public house on Nabbs Lane, a provocative stone's throw from Slaithwaite church (the landlord had also fallen out with the local establishment having temporarily lost his licence) before the Pole Moor Chapel was built.

The Pole Moor congregation were Particular Baptists: strict in their Calvinist belief that they were an elect predestined to be saved. Successive pastors seem to have varied in the fierceness of their preaching.

The second, Charles Bamford, a convert, was described by Sykes (1906) as being a hyper-Calvinist. He adhered to the doctrine of eternal adoption and eternal justification, according to which every human being was destined from their beginning to eternal bliss or eternal woe, according to the unquestionable will of an all-wise Creator, the individual's '... own will, his own deeds or shortcomings, availing not one jot to try by a hair's breadth the original scheme of creation.' Those who spoke of salvation through repentance and amended life were '... rotten, weak-minded, illogical, benighted, corrupt seducers from the faith'. Such fierce, binary, preaching was evidently common at the time. To a modern ear it has echoes in the religious leadership styles that have emerged during other times when sectarian and political divides have reinforced each other, as in the Northern Ireland of the late twentieth century.

Bamford's congregation was evidently divided, between those who believed as he did and were thus members of an exclusive elect, and 'Fullerists', followers of Andrew Fuller (1754–1815) who favoured a more outward-looking, evangelical, faith into which outsiders might convert. According to Sykes (1906) this division continued unresolved throughout the first fifteen years of the nineteenth century. It became less fierce after Abraham Webster (the pastor who features in *Ben O'Bills*) took over the flock in 1808. Pastor Webster is described as a 'pleasant and feeling speaker, and very kind and charitable minded'. It is perhaps a mark of his empathy for his congregation that he evidently relished the small holding attached to his lodgings where '... he might be found any week day, shod in clogs, dressed in home-spun, spreading dung, cleansing the shippon, or missal, or foddering his beasts'.

Even so, seven of the Pole Moor congregation left to start what became the Providence Baptist Chapel, founded in 1816 in Hollins Row, in the valley bottom near the centre of Slaithwaite but, again, just over the Dartmouth estate boundary, this time in Linthwaite. It was known locally as the 'Strict and Particular' or 'Gadsby's' after Fuller's sternest critic, William Gadsby (1773–1844).

Webster moved to Hebden Bridge in 1818 and was succeeded by Lawrence Shaw, who seems to have taken a vehement but erratic line. According to Sykes (1906) he at first described adherents of Arminianism and Fullerism as false prophets peddling damnable heresies. He sought to sift them from the congregation but, just, failed to do so. By 1822 he retained his vehement and confrontational approach but had switched his allegiance to the Arminians' side. Challenged by his old, Calvinist, allies he ex-communicated at first ten of them, and then a further fifteen. The membership of the Providence Chapel's community of Strict and Particular Baptists, grew as a result. Shortly afterwards Abraham Webster was invited back and tempers seem to have mellowed.

What is striking about this period is the intensity of the divisions. To those involved the doctrinal issues were clearly powerful - they were, after all, about salvation and about group identity. But they seem also to reflect the more general fervour of the times. This was the period when the state was most wary of the radicalism of the French Revolution spreading to English soil, when Thomas Paine was read aloud in cells of workers affected by the economic downturn that accompanied the Napoleonic wars, when the seeds that sprouted into the Chartist movement of the mid-century were germinating. The same Colne Valley textile workers who formed the early Baptist congregations were also affected by the wider social fomentations.

Legacy of Baptist chapels and Sunday schools in the landscape

Whatever the tenor of the times, the combination of industrialisation, population growth, and vigour in the Baptist movement has left a handsome set of buildings in prominent settings on the valley sides.

Sunnybank Chapel, illustrated at the start of this section, is one of two on Bolster Moor. The other lies, appropriately enough, on Meeting House Lane. That they were built within thirty years of each other, with the later chapel much larger than the first, gives a sense of the scale of the expansion of the Baptist congregations in the second half of the nineteenth century.

There was a parallel expansion less than a mile away at Scapegoat Hill. A new outpost from the Bolster Moor chapel was established on Scapegoat Hill High Street in 1849, to be succeeded by the much larger complex of Church and School, on what became School Lane, in the 1870s. And there was yet another Baptist building just round the flank of Wholestone Hill at Round Ings Road, built in 1876.

Dropping down to just beyond Golcar Town End there was a further succession of chapels just off Brook Lane. The first was built in 1835 by

Thomas Sykes, who was a member of the Salendine Nook Baptist Community. It was re-built in the 1860s, and then converted into a Sunday School as a larger chapel was built close by in the 1890s. It is the Sunday School and the Chapel Manse that survive.

The last-built of the chapels, the Zion Baptist Chapel which opened as a school and chapel at Hilltop in 1891, was the only one which was built within the Slaithwaite parish boundary. By then the industrial development and terraced housing along the valley floor had already loosened the grip of the Dartmouth Estate and the Anglican church.

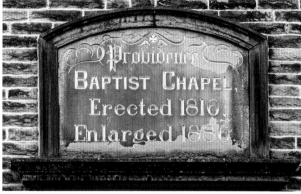

FIGS. 52–56.

Top Left and Right: Providence Baptist Chapel, first built in 1816 by Strict Baptists breaking away from the Pole Moor congregation.

Middle Left: Clough Head Baptist Chapel, built on the edge of Crimble Clough in 1866, now a private house (SE 0831 1565).

Middle Right: Scapegoat Hill Church, 1871. The largest on the hillside, and still active.

Bottom Left: Golcar Baptist Sunday school.

So, in a period of just over a century, the settlements on the hillside to the North of Slaithwaite, but beyond the parish boundary, had gained from the development of nine Baptist chapels, of which seven are still standing and continuing to provide a dignified presence amongst the stone terraces. The community had grown from a small group meeting in the upstairs room of a pub to one that filled chapels with a combined capacity of several thousand.

Methodism in the Valley

By the end of the nineteenth century there were as many Methodist chapels in the Valley, but they are less visible in the broad sweep of the landscape. The individual chapels are large, handsome and imposing, but they were built within the expanding industrial communities that were spreading along the valley bottoms and the lower slopes.

During John Wesley's lifetime Methodism was a revivalist movement within the established Church of England. He had been ordained as an Anglican priest and remained one, despite tensions, throughout his life. His was an intense faith, in part a reaction to the rather degraded state of the established church in the eighteenth century, but then further focused by engagement with the quiet spiritual force of the Arminian Moravian movement in America, where he preached in his thirties. His driving evangelism is said to have followed an experience, during a Lutheran church service in Aldersgate in London, that

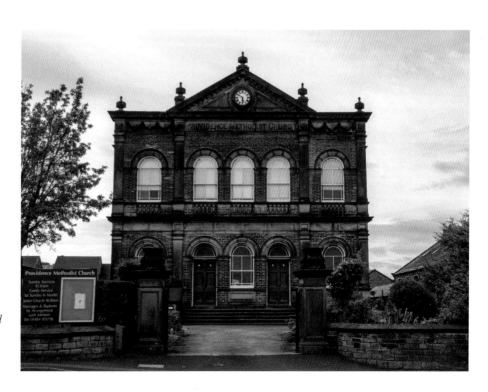

FIG. 57.
Providence Methodist Church, Golcar, built in the 1880s. Note the characteristic pair of entrance doors. Wesley favoured the separation of the sexes, but the form here is perhaps more about architectural balance.

rooted in him a commitment to personal salvation through faith. He began his lifelong commitment to preaching, often several times a day, and often in the open air in early decades, in the late 1730s.

Famously, he was taken aback by the Huddersfield population he encountered in 1757:

> I rode over the mountains to Huddersfield. A wilder people I never saw in England. The men, women and children filled the streets and seemed just ready to devour us.

He will have passed through the Colne Valley on his route.

But the experience seems to have served only to increase his missionary resolve. Throughout the 1760s he preached frequently in Huddersfield and the neighbouring valleys. He made common cause, and a strong friendship, with Henry Venn, the vicar who reformed and invigorated the Huddersfield Anglican Church. Venn himself was an evangeliser, much inspired by Wesley and Methodism. *The Annals of the Church in Slaithwaite* record that 'He was a man of mighty power, "A burning and a shining light"'. (Hulbert, 1864)

According to Sykes (1906), Venn had been appointed to the Huddersfield parish by Sir John Ramsden on the recommendation of the Earl of Dartmouth, who evidently supported the Methodist movement. It was not he but one of his successors, the Fourth Earl, who collaborated with the Church of England in the Valley to push Baptism to the margins, but their family's attitudes to Methodism would have been very different in any case. The movement was part of the Church of England, and revitalising it rather than competing with it. It did not emphasise the separation of the saved as the Calvinist Baptist movement did. And its core tenet of salvation through personal faith and direct relationship with God did not provide a reinforcing link to the drive for social and political reform that so worried the establishment through much of the nineteenth century. In E. P. Thomson's powerful characterisation, Methodism was the 'chiliasm of despair' (Thompson, 1963). In his analysis it encouraged too much acceptance of the existing social and economic hierarchy; it diverted attention from current injustices to prospects of salvation beyond the grave; it accepted 'sacerdotal' authority from its priests, rather than developing the collective voice of the congregation. It was, in short, no threat to the established order, and its chapels and churches were thus welcome in the parish and on the Dartmouth estate.

In the event Methodist chapel building did not get underway until the early decades of the nineteenth century. Wesley and his followers were first to be found preaching in Anglican churches or, quite often, to outdoor assemblies of followers. Wesley himself seems to have had extraordinary stamina alongside his evangelising convictions. Sykes (1906) reports that on one July day in 1772 he preached in Halifax at 4am, in Netherthong at 10am, in Huddersfield at 2pm, and in Dewsbury in the evening: twenty five miles of travelling, presumably on horseback, as well as four services.

As distinct Methodist groups began to form they, like the early Baptists in the Valley, met in private homes and pubs. Sykes records a group at the Rose and Crown at Cop Hill. There was a group using a converted house at the bottom of Fall Lane in Marsden, and one at Lower Wood at Lingards. And, again like the early Baptists, there were tensions between those in the congregations who were committed to evangelism, and those who perhaps favoured a more traditional style of preaching. Hulbert's *Annals* (1864) record the experience of John Murgatroyd, 'a tall and venerable looking man, who wore a powdered wig and a long cloak'. He was a curate in the Almondbury parish in 1779 and his diary records his attempts to preach at Marsden:

> March the 28th, at Marsden, and the Chapel-warden, encouraged by the Methodistical party, kept the door locked again, so we'd no service. ... The 11th, The chapel door locked again . ... April the 25th. At Marsden and the door locked still. As I went up three or four men were placed in Mr Marsden's wood to abuse me, who did so in a shameful manner.

John Wesley died in 1791, and the Methodist movement drew away from the Church of England, forming separate governance structures and building its own chapels during a period of rapid expansion. There were 250 such

FIG. 58.
The Methodist Chapel, Sunday School, and hall in Linthwaite.

chapels completed in England in the 1780s, more than ten times that number in the 1810s.

The first purpose built Wesleyan chapel in the Valley was in Linthwaite, completed in 1810. By the late nineteenth century the communities that had grown up around the mills along the valley bottom were supporting seven Methodist Chapels and Churches, from Parkwood, in Longwood, to Marsden, and they had become larger and more imposing as the century had progressed.

The 1810 chapel has now gone, but the strength of Methodism in the Linthwaite community by mid-century is evident from the cluster of churches, chapels, schools and halls that are a major presence in the village. The population of Linthwaite increased fivefold as the industrial development of the Valley progressed through the nineteenth century, reaching just under 7000 by the end of the century. The legacy of buildings makes clear the strength of Methodism through the period of the community's growth. The grouping of church, school and hall has presence in the settlement, and in Linthwaite it is the Church of England, not the Non-Conformists, which occupies a site higher up the valley side, at Broad Oak.

The Church of England revitalised - new churches, missions and Sunday schools

In spite of their numbers, their chapels and Sunday schools, the Valley's Non-Conformists did not have it all their own way. The established church put up a spirited resistance and, although marginally fewer, its buildings in the landscape reflect that.

The Linthwaite church, Christ Church, was one of two built by the Church Buildings Commission in the 1820s. The other is St John's at Golcar. They are both 'Waterloo' churches, built using state funds after the end of the Napoleonic Wars, to ensure that the Church of England had a presence in the expanding towns and cities. In part it was to make sure that allegiances of those populations were not ceded to Non-Conformism, and perhaps also to radical political thought. They were funded by the 'Million Pounds Act' of 1818, topped up by a further half million in 1824.

Slaithwaite's chapel had been replaced by the much larger St James Church at the end of the eighteenth century, and the fine St Bartholomew's Church, 'the Cathedral of the Valley', had replaced Marsden's chapel by the end of the nineteenth century.

By the late nineteenth century the revitalised Church of England in the Valley was also competing with the Baptist and Methodists chapels on the valley sides. They were establishing outposts: missions and Sunday schools.

In his *Annals of the Church in Slaithwaite* (1864) Charles Hulbert, the ally of the fourth Earl in his attempts to sustain the old social and economic

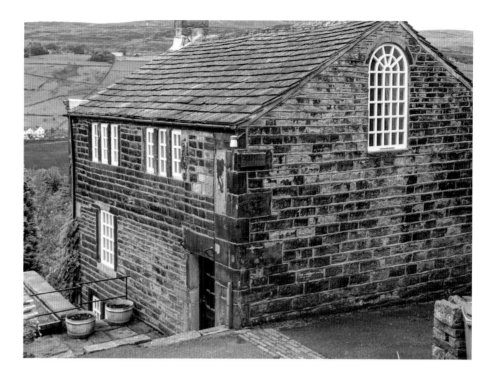

FIG. 59.
The Sunday School building at Bank Nook, on the hillside above West Slaithwaite (SE 0600 1322).

order in the Valley, notes tussles over the education of the young in particular. He reports the efforts of one of his predecessors, in the 1820s, to establish an Anglican Sunday school:

> An attempt was also made by Mr. Jackson to establish a Sunday School at Cophill, on what is called the Holm side of Slaithwaite; indicating his sense of the necessities of that part of the Chapelry, ... But he met with little success and much opposition, even insult; owing to the prevalence of dissent in that neighbourhood. But, on his withdrawal, there resulted the formation of a Sunday School at 'Bank Nook,' which still exists; professedly conducted upon the principle of 'No particular form of Religion'; but actually carried on by the Particular Baptists of the Secession party.

Hulbert adds:

> In making these records of facts, which I cannot but deplore, in their tendency to separate and divide Christ's Church, I must he understood to bear testimony to the individual piety of many members of dissenting communities; and my joy in any real good which they may effect.

However sincere the Rev Hulbert was in this last sentiment, competition between the established and Non-Conformist churches became more vigorous as the nineteenth century went on. It seems to have focused particularly, and perhaps appropriately, on the early engagement of the children of the

Valley through Sunday schools. Many of the Baptist and Methodist chapels had Sunday schools by mid-century. The Church of England feared that it was losing future generations from its congregations and began to promote alternatives. The first were attached to the churches in the valley bottom, but by the 1840s they were being built amongst the Non-Conformist chapels high on the hillsides. There they remain in the landscape - some still in use, some adapted to other purposes, and one at Hill Top on Lingards Lane on the South side of the Valley above Slaithwaite, now in disrepair.

In his first Decennial report the Rev Hulbert's records the opening of the first of the hillside buildings, the Sunday School on the Meltham Road at Holthead. The school opened with thirty-four pupils, but quickly doubled its numbers despite its isolation. But it seems to have operated for only seven years before the focus moved to the newly built National School in Marsden.

The revitalised Church of England turned its attention to the northern side of the Valley, where, as Rev Hulbert reports, there was 'a very poor and ignorant population' who lived too far from the church in the valley to attend regularly. The community living close to Pole Moor seem to have been particularly wild:

FIG. 60.
The Sunday School at Holthead, opened in 1840. Now a private house. (SE 0807 1204).

FIG. 61.

Shred Mission, opened in 1845 and still serving much the same purposes of family worship and early learning, although not with the same numbers as Rev Hulbert reported in the 1850s, when 150 attended each Sunday and 50-60 scholars each weekday.

That wild and mountainous region was the congenial home, or retreat, of the uncouth Burntplatters, a class of semi-barbarous people, possible of gypsy origin, who live in mean hovels, herded together like cattle, defying all law, alike human and divine, and subsisting by poaching, hawking, theft, and anyhow rather than by honest industry. (Sykes, 1906)

(Sykes also bases his 1908 novel, *Miriam*, on the developing relationship between a young woman, apparently one of the Burntplatters but in fact the daughter of a Greek-reading estranged teacher living as a hermit on Marsden Moor, and Abel, a son of the minister at Pole Moor Chapel.)

The Earl of Dartmouth gave land for what became the Shred Mission on Bradshaw Lane. Here there has been continuity – the Shred community still hold services once a month, and a pre-school uses the premises.

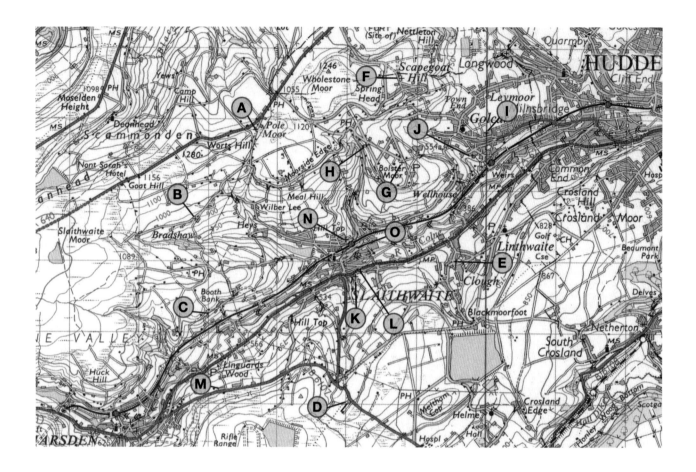

FIG. 62.

Chapels and Sunday Schools: locations

A   *Pole Moor Chapel*
B   *Shred Mission*
C   *Bank Nook Sunday School*
D   *Holt Head Sunday School*
E   *Linthwaite Methodist buildings*
F   *Scapegoat Hill Church*
G   *Sunnybank Chapel*
H   *Clough Head Baptist Chapel*
I   *Providence Methodist Church*
J   *Golcar Sunday School*
K   *Providence Baptist Chapel*
L   *Slaithwaite Centenary Methodist Chapel*
M   *Lingards Sunday School*

CONNECTIONS

JUST AS THE landscape of the Valley has been formed by its topography and social history, so too have been the networks that evolved to enable its necessary connections – through the Valley to the world beyond; from houses to the fields and common grazing; from workshop to workshop; from homes to churches and chapels; from the hillsides to the industrial settlements along the valley bottom.

The cumulative result is a rich layering of local tracks over the strong vectors of the routes which run along the corridor of the valley and up over (or under) Standedge, the narrowest crossing of the South Pennine watershed. Few parts of the country have such wealth of walking routes. They are strong visual elements in the landscape – and they make that landscape particularly accessible.

FIG. 63.

The head of the green lane that drops down towards Marsden from Cop Hill.

The Colne Valley corridor

The evidence of Mesolithic and Bronze Age activity in the Valley is on the highest ground, as it is in much of the English landscape. The valleys were wet, thickly forested and potentially dangerous. On the hills life was safer, and travel easier.

But if there is visual evidence of early trackways along the Colne Valley corridor it is indirect. It may well be that routes along the watersheds which are still in use follow pathways that would have made the same sense five millennia ago as they do now, but that can only be a supposition. And such suppositions can turn out to be wrong.

The Roman road

It has long been known that there was a Roman road between Chester and York, and that the stretch between the forts at Castleshaw, near Delph, and Slack, on the western edge of Outlane, must have passed along the Colne Valley. Its route up through Saddleworth is known, reaching the top of the Pennine escarpment at Millstone Edge, above Thieves Clough. The assumption was that having reached the high ground, above the thickets and the marshes, the Romans would have kept to it by then turning North, along Standedge, to then curve to the East and follow the watershed over March Haigh and Cupwith hills and along the route of what is now the A640 as it gently descends to Pole Moor and on to Slack. (That stretch of the A640 is beguilingly straight – it *looks* like a Roman road.) That is the line described by Crump (1949) in his work on Huddersfield highways, and indeed by Ian Richmond, the pre-eminent historian of Roman Britain of the mid-twentieth century. But we now know that they were both mistaken.

In 1973 the farmer of land at Moorside Edge asked a friend who was a leading member of the Huddersfield and District Archaeological Society (HDAS) for his opinion of a faint linear bank running across his field. The trench that was opened up that autumn found a Roman road just 25cm below the surface. It was well-engineered: small cobbles were laid on flat stones to form a cambered section 7.5m wide, with substantial ditches on either side. It had been built on the surface of the land to form a raised 'agger'. It was in fact a classic Roman construction.

That first find opened up a long quest by the HDAS. In 1982 they explored a linear terrace on the South-east slope of Pule Hill and again found a roadway, this one overlaid by a packhorse causeway. They postulated routes which joined the three known points – Moorside Edge, Pule Hill, and the Millstone Edge cutting – and probed the ground. By the end of the 1980s they had found the road, and the footing of what may have been a watch or signalling tower at Worlow, at the highest point of the route as it skirted Pule Hill above

FIG. 64.

The faint line of the Roman Road across Moorside Edge is visible in this aerial photograph, copied from the 'Roman Roads Research Association Gazetteer' (it is route 712). In the right light conditions the agger can still be made out if you look down from the Rocking Stones edge of Wholestone Hill.

FIG. 65.

A cross-section of the road excavated at Upper Holme by HDAS in 1988 (from 'The Romans came this way', 2008).

67

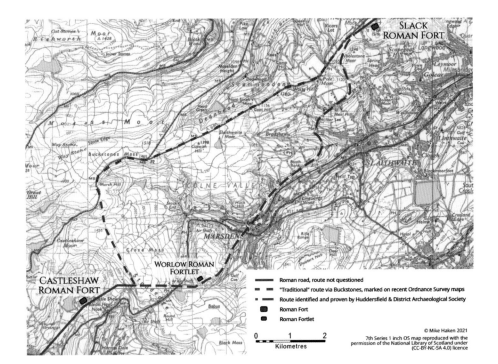

Roman road, route not questioned
"Traditional" route via Buckstones, marked on recent Ordnance Survey maps
Route identified and proven by Huddersfield & District Archaeological Society
Roman Fort
Roman Fortlet

© Mike Haken 2021
7th Series 1 inch OS map reproduced with the permission of the National Library of Scotland under (CC-BY-NC-SA 4.0) licence

FIG. 66.
The route of the Roman Road from Castleshaw to Slack – as long assumed, and then as established by the work of HDAS.

FIG. 67.
Slaithwaite Manor House with the Dial Stone (right foreground) – thought to have been a Roman Milestone and originally located at Booth Bank.

Old Mount Road; a particularly fine section at Upper Holme; and evidence of a river crossing point at Clough House Bridge in Merrydale. In the 1990s they found the road again as it ran from the East side of Redbrook Reservoir up to Thieves Bridge – this time in a linear depression where the road builders had dug down through the peat and based their construction on the bedrock. Emergency digs as builders stood by found sections at West Top and Nursery Nook along Moorside Edge, and the route of the final section round the West flank of Wholestone Moor was confirmed by probing the line up to Rochdale Road.

The story of HDAS's work is one of evidence, reasoned speculation, investigation yielding more evidence – and of persistence and the delights of discovery and vindication. It is well told in their book, *The Romans came this way* (2008). Their achievement is a proven line from Millstone Edge – not along the watershed to the North, but down past Thieves Bridge, around the South side of Pule Hill, through Marsden, and then diagonally up to Moorside Edge before skirting Wholestone Moor.

And the Colne Valley may have a Roman Milestone, in the 'Diall Stone' now to be found in the grounds of Slaithwaite Manor House, but first described in the sixteenth century at Booth Bank, on the line up to Upper Holme.

Monastic records

The excavated sections show the Roman road to have been impressively well built. It must surely have continued in use long after the Romans themselves withdrew at the end of the fourth century. Certainly the Colne Valley continued to be part of important long distance routes across the Pennines.

Crump (1949) draws on twelfth and thirteenth century Cistercian records to provide evidence of the monastic ways through the Valley. These routes connected monastic holdings to the abbeys, and were also used to bring salt and other materials from further afield, in the case of salt, from the Cheshire plains.

David Hey (2001) makes clear the significance of the salt trade. He quotes the *Victorian County History of Staffordshire's* calculation that 100 packhorses a week were carrying salt from Cheshire to Derbyshire along the route through Leek. Crump reports evidence in thirteenth century Fountains Abbey records of a similar traffic through the Colne Valley, along much the same long distance corridor as the Roman road. The trade was important enough to bequeath names to tracks and junctions along the way. There was a Salterhebble bridge at Delph, on the Lancashire side of Standedge, and Salterhebble remains the name for both the bridge over the Calder and the stretch of the canal on the way up to Halifax. Both lay on the route between Halifax and Marsden which is indicated by an eighteenth century guide stoop on Lindley Moor Road, itself referred to as 'Saltergate' in the abbey records.

Packhorse trails

Some of the corridor routes recorded in monastic records are still in use, in part no doubt because they follow obvious lines along the watersheds and down to river crossings. But, if the Hoskins landscape history discipline is anchored in features that are still *visible* in the modern landscape, the highways and tracks that properly meet the test are the packhorse trails.

These trails became increasingly well-engineered in the service of a growing wool trade from the fifteenth century onwards. The trade needed access to markets. As the scale of production grew, not just in the Valley but beyond it to the other West Riding towns, the clothiers ceased carrying their lengths on their own backs and turned to packhorses. The scale of the packhorse traffic required the rough tracks to be paved, particularly where they crossed water and scaled steep ground. They were commonly laid with 'causeys' – rough flags that allowed pedestrians to avoid the mud.

It is these packhorse trails that survive as strong features in the Colne Valley landscape. The best known runs up over Standedge from Eastergate, just beyond Hey Green to the West of Marsden.

Eastergate takes its name not from the Christian festival, but from 'Esther's Gate'. Esther evidently kept a hostelry just beyond the bridge. It will have been a welcome sight for those coming down from the moors above, and a last point of call for those heading the other way. Crump dates the bridge as seventeenth or eighteenth century. It is close to a ford across the upper reaches of the Colne.

FIG. 68.
The causey track along the route on the South side of the Valley, above Lingards (SE 0676 1267).

FIG. 69.
Close Gate Bridge at Eastergate, Marsden.

FIG. 70.

The packhorse route from Marsden to Pole Moor. The bridge is in Merrydale, at the foot of Tyas Lane (SE 0584 1427).

From Eastergate the packhorse road runs up over Close Moor to Buckstones, across the Pennine watershed, and down to Rochdale. In the other direction it was the route to Halifax, an important centre for the wool trade before Huddersfield began to develop. The route went through Marsden, up past Slaithwaite Hall, where a green lane still runs up towards Cop Hill, across to another stone bridge in Merrydale, and then up to the edge of the Valley at Pole Moor.

The A640 to Rochdale (which follows the route of an early nineteenth century turnpike, described below) and the M62 both cut through Pole Moor, hard by the Lower Royal George. But the older packhorse route across the Pennines via Marsden is still indicated on a guide stoop close to the pub (fig. 71). According to Crump (1949) guide stoops were required by a law of 1698 wherever there was a significant junction of tracks. There is further example, dated 1756, near Scapegoat Hill, where several lanes still meet on the edge of Longwood Common (fig. 72).

Turnpikes

In his introduction to the *The Age of Revolution* (1962), the first of his great quartet of European histories, Eric Hobsbawm sets the scene of Europe in the late eighteenth century. He describes the transformation in communications that came as economic growth led to a scale of trade which required transport by cart rather than packhorse, and of a fourfold increase of speed for those making journeys using new carriage services. Between 1760 and 1800 the time taken to travel from London to Glasgow fell from twelve days to sixty-two hours.

It was a revolution in highway construction that made these developments possible – the coming of an age of turnpikes. They were made both necessary and economically viable by the early industrial revolution, and that first took root either side of the South Pennines. It is thus striking but not surprising that

FIG. 71.

The guide stoop at the Lower Royal George.
(SE 0696 1631). The elegantly cuffed hands
point to:
* *Halifax, 5 Miles*
* *Huddersfield, 5 Miles, and*
* *Scammonden and Deanhead*
It names the surveyor – John Wodhed – and
is dated 1755.

FIG. 72.

The guide stoop near Scapegoat Hill.
(SE 0859 1673). It indicates:
* *Rippond[en] 3 Mile*
* *Halifax 4 Mile*
* *Slaighwai[te] 2 Mile*

there are two significant turnpike routes though the Colne Valley corridor, and that one of those routes took three sequential forms as trade increased.

Looking towards Lancashire from Pule Hill, above Marsden, the successive routes of the Wakefield to Austerlands turnpike are still evident in the roads and tracks across the Standedge moorland. The first two turnpikes passed to the South of the hill, the third to the North.

Austerlands lies on the North-east edge of Lees, near Oldham. Its billing as a turnpike destination was a consequence of the delayed commitment to the Manchester to Wakefield route on the Yorkshire side of the moors. The Parliamentary Acts which empowered turnpike companies to create the new highways, and then to collect the tolls which made them financially viable (at least in prospect), were promoted county by county. It was the Manchester interests that first proposed a route across the Pennines to Wakefield. Their

Act was passed in 1735, and the road through Oldham to the (then) county edge at Austerlands was completed soon afterwards. The Yorkshire interests only followed through with an Act to enable the remaining route, from Wakefield to Austerlands, in 1758.

The early turnpikes followed established routes. The intent was to upgrade a degraded track to become an engineered highway which would allow the passage of wheeled traffic in all weathers. Crump (1949) quotes from the typically verbose preamble to the Wakefield to Austerlands Act:

> Whereas the Road leading from the town of Wakefield (W.R. of York) thro' the towns of Horbury, Netherton, Overton, Lepton, Almondbury, Huddersfield, Marsden and Saddleworth to Austerlands in the said county, being situated in a trading and populous Part of the same County, and much used and frequented for the Carriage and Conveyance of Goods, Wares and Merchandise, Commodities and Provisions, made, manufactured and consumed in that Country and so necessary to be made passable and kept in Repair for the preserving

FIG. 73.

From Pule Hill looking towards Manchester. The first Wakefield to Austerlands turnpike followed the line of the current tarmac road that runs diagonally from Mount Bar towards Gilberts and then across the A62 (which runs along the route of the third turnpike at that stage) and on to Thieves Bridge. The second turnpike is still present as the well-engineered track, visible here, running above the left side of Carr Clough up towards the Standedge cutting, just right of centre on the horizon.

and encouragement the Trade and Commerce thereof, is, from the Narrowness and Steepness thereof in many Places and the nature of the Soil, become so deep and ruinous that in Winter and Wet-Seasons the same is almost impassable for Wheel Carriages …, etc… .

The upgraded highway followed the line of the current Meltham to Marsden road, past Badger Gate (a badger was a travelling salesman), to Town Gate in Marsden. From there it followed what is still called Old Mount Road, rising steadily to Mount Bar, and then via Gilberts to cross the marshy ground at the top of the moor to Thieves Bridge and on to reach Standedge before dropping down to Austerlands.

It was built by John Metcalfe, 'Blind Jack', of Knaresborough, the most famous of the turnpike engineers. He it was who established a means of crossing marshy ground that eschewed the time-consuming and costly effort of excavating down to bedrock (as the Romans had done across the same marshy ground either side of Thieves Bridge) in favour of building the highway on rafts of brushwood and ling laid on the surface of the peat. His approach allowed him to put in a low tender for the work, but was sceptically received. Crump (1949) quotes from the narrative of Metcalfe's life published by Edward Peck in 1812:

Numbers of clothiers usually going that way to Huddersfield market were not sparing in their censure, and held much diversity of opinion relative to its completion; but Metcalfe got the piece levelled to the end, having sixty men employed there, he ordered them to pull and bind heather, or ling, in round bundles and to lay it on the intended road in rows, and laying another across, pressing them well down: he then brought broad wheeled carriages … to lead stone and gravel for covering. When the first load was laid, and the horses had gone off in safety, the company huzzared from surprise: they completed the whole of its length, which was about half a mile; and it was so particularly fine that any person might have gone over it in winter unshod, without being wet. This piece of road needed no repairs for twelve years afterwards.

The completion of the first turnpike seems to have had a transformative impact on the people of Marsden. The following year saw the installation of pews in the newly built church there. They had been made across the moors in Saddleworth and were transported to Marsden by cart. Hulbert (1864), the then vicar, reports that his parishioners flocked to meet the cart bringing them to the village, to welcome the pews, but also to 'behold the wonderful conveyance, for a cart or wagon had never before been seen in Marsden'.

There may be some hyperbole there, but it is certainly true that the opening up of a reliable wheeled traffic was a significant factor in the growth of textile trade in the late eighteenth and early nineteenth centuries, in the Valley and across the wider West Riding. An earlier section has described its increasing reach in the eighteenth century. The scale and form of both the Huddersfield Cloth Hall and the Halifax Piece Hall, built in 1766 and 1779 respectively, were testaments to its commercial confidence. The turnpikes were an enabling component in the manufacturing and trading systems that powered the take-off of the industrial economy in the South Pennines.

As traffic increased expectations became more demanding and by the last quarter of the eighteenth century the turnpike trustees drove a new route taking a more gently climbing line up what is now New Mount Road to Mount Bar. This second turnpike went on across the moor, to the South of Redbrook this time, on a line which allowed a steadier gradient to Standedge. The second turnpike still provides a well-engineered and dry track across the moor.

The third Wakefield to Austerlands turnpike was made in the 1820s, and took an entirely new route close to the developing mills and settlements of the valley bottom before going to the North of Pule Hill, on the other side from the first and second routes, and up across the moor to the newly made Standedge cutting. It is the route of the current A62 Manchester Road – the 'arterial route' before the M62 was made.

The entirely separate Huddersfield to New Hey Turnpike was created by an act of 1806, connecting West Yorkshire to Rochdale, which lies just beyond New Hey. This is the route of the A640 which runs from Outlane through Pole Moor and up to Buckstones – finally establishing a road along the northern watershed of the valley that was once assumed to be the route of

FIG. 74.
The third turnpike, now the A62, taking what was then a new route to the North of Pule Hill up to Gilberts and then on to the Standedge cutting.

the Roman road. Its place in the Colne Valley landscape is thus on its margin, but often too on its skyline where it acts as a reminder to the walker of a faster moving world.

Canal and railway

The interests of landowners and mill developers that came together to develop the turnpikes were also represented in the company of 1793 that promoted the Huddersfield Narrow Canal from Aspley Basin to Portland Basin in Ashton-under-Lyne. and that company went on to be incorporated fifty years later into the Huddersfield and Manchester Railway and Canal Company. All were driven by the need to transport freight, raw materials and finished goods, in greater and greater bulk, more and more reliably, and preferably at greater speed. Their stories are well told in Graham Keevill's *Standedge Guide* (1986), *Pennine Passage* by Michael and Peter Fox (1991), and *The Standedge Tunnels* by Trevor Ellis (2017).

The project to construct the canal started with ambition and confidence. The challenge of driving a three mile tunnel under the Pennine backbone using late eighteenth century techniques was first assessed in 1793 by Nicholas Brown, the surveyor employed by the newly-formed Huddersfield Canal Company. His view was that:

> the hill through which the Tunnel is to be made appears favourable, the strata consists of gritstone and strong shale, and the low ground in the centre near Red-Brook will afford an opportunity for opening

FIG. 75.
Tunnel End.
The spillway feeding the canal crosses over the railway in front of the tunnel entrances.

FIG. 76.
Towers above the ventilation shafts at Pule Holes (SE 0300 1076).

the works by means of steam engines, so as to greatly facilitate the completion of the Tunnel, which I conceive may be accomplished in five years. (Quoted in Ellis, 2017)

That proved to be an optimistic prospectus. Nicholas Brown was dismissed in 1798 after an independent survey found that 'The masonry and earth work of this canal were the worst executed of any I ever saw.' That assessment was followed by a further setback when much of the early work on the line through Marsden was undermined by a major flood in 1799. It was also discovered that the line of the tunnel strayed both vertically and horizontally. There is a still an 'S' bend in the tunnel below the Redbrook shaft to accommodate a discrepancy of 27 feet. In the end it was eighteen years until the canal opened in 1811, and the end of the 1830s before its shareholders began to receive dividends. By then the railway age had arrived and further tunnels were being planned.

The railway construction went more smoothly. The first Act authorising the line from Leeds through Huddersfield to Manchester, crucially supported by the Ramsden estate which owned the bulk of the freeholds in Huddersfield, was passed in 1844 and the first single-track tunnel under Standedge was opened by 1849. That one is straight: it is said that you can see daylight from one end to the other, 5000 metres away on the other side of the Pennine moors. The second single track tunnel was opened in 1871 and the final double track tunnel in 1894.

The railway tracks are valley bottom features and their contribution to the landscape of the valley sides is essentially as part of the visual backdrop rather than in the foreground. But that changes as they pass under Pule Hill and Standedge. Here the line of the tunnels is marked on the surface by substantial engine houses and ventilation towers. They stand above shafts

FIG. 77.
*Engine House at Redbrook
(SE 0264 1032).*

used to allow the first railway tunnel workings to be driven from multiple faces. Cross adits to the canal tunnel allowed spoil to be removed. There are three shafts with a significant presence in landscape above Marsden, at Pule Hill, Pule Holes and Red Brook. All were equipped first with Newcomen steam engines to lift men and spoil from the tunnel workings. Later small reservoirs and conduits were constructed to allow the steam engines to be replaced by water-balance engines, thus ending the expense of bringing in large quantities of coal along the turnpike (Ellis, 2017). The Redbrook shaft, reservoir, and water channels are the most substantial structures and the most easily accessible.

Hobsbawm's *Age of Revolution* (1962) covers a period of just fifty-nine years, from 1789 to 1848. It is a striking manifestation of the industrial revolution in the South Pennines that over an only slightly longer period transport through the Colne Valley evolved from packhorse trails, through sequential turnpikes and a canal, to the railway and arterial roads. As you take in the view from almost anywhere on the valley sides one or another of these, and often two or more, will be in view – reminding you of the significance of the Valley as a corridor, and of the industrial history that drove forward the local economy and settlement pattern.

Local tracks

The corridor routes are visually significant, but there is a second set of connections which are at least as strong as defining characteristics of the Valley. It has a great wealth of tracks connecting local places: farmstead to

FIG. 78.
*This walled track runs from
Butterley up to Binn Edge, in
the Wessenden Valley
(SE 0495 1063).*

FIG. 79.
This track takes you down from Westwood Edge and Bolster Moor to Slaithwaite. It is known to generations of children as Spider Alley. It is beautifully made (SE 0849 1466).

farmstead, hillside settlement to valley floor, routes to the chapels on the hillsides, routes to the fields and the moor-top open grazing, tracks to bring stone down from the quarries in the high strata of millstone grit and ganister. There are few landscapes with such a highly developed network of walking tracks, and many of them are strikingly well made.

The particular richness of the connections is rooted in the dispersed settlement pattern and the long history of the dual textile and farming economy. The manorial rolls of the sixteenth and seventeenth centuries have several entries that make clear the importance of tracks, and the responsibilities of the householder for the maintenance of those that pass over their land. Many were used for moving cattle to the fields, and many remain well-walled to this day.

By the mid nineteenth century, many hillside families were working in the new mills along the valley floor. Some of the routes that took them down from their homes are particularly well made, possibly testaments to the combination of the availability of labour during periods of economic depression, the interests of the industrialists, and possibly also to the philanthropy of the Dartmouth Earls who created work schemes draining land and building new roads.

It is the combination of long distance routes and a rich reticule of well-made local tracks that makes for a major element of the Colne Valley landscape. They are visually striking, both as foreground features and as lines in the more distant pattern of fields and walls.

They are always purposeful – or at least they have always had purpose. Inevitably some have fallen into disuse. There are some that have become stream-beds in winter, and some that have now have little footfall and have become neglected and overgrown. But a high proportion are still used by hillside residents going about their business. They still need and use the connections.

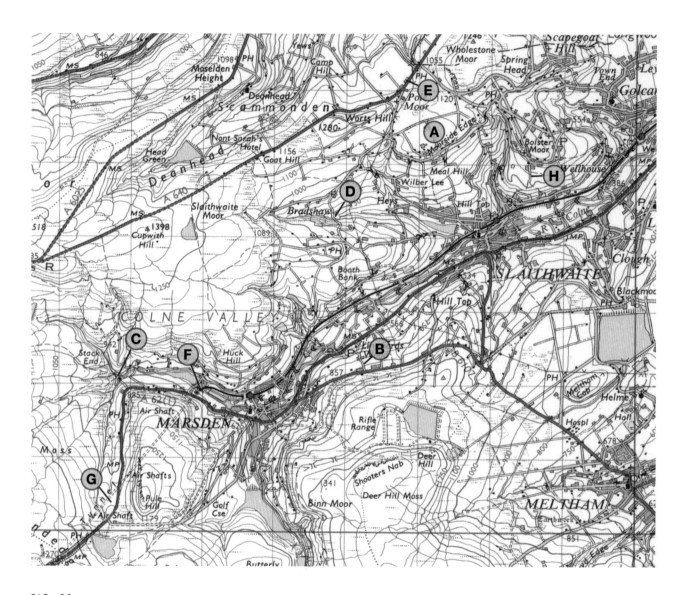

FIG. 80.

Connections: locations

A. *Moorside Edge*
B. *Causey stones, above Lingards*
C. *Eastergate Packhorse Bridge*
D. *Tyas Lane bridge, Merrydale*
E. *Lower Royal George*
F. *Tunnel End*
G. *Redbrook Engine House*
H. *Spider Alley*

WATER

AS MANY A walker who has come down from the moors at the end of the day will know, the beers brewed in Marsden are named after reservoirs: March Haigh, Redbrook, Butterley. That is as it should be. Reservoirs and conduits, dams and bridges, are often points of reference for journeys on foot through the Valley, and they catch the light and reflect the weather whenever you look to the horizon.

The Pennine watershed has a high rainfall and the strata of millstone grit lie over bands of impervious shale, so that springs are common and they flow consistently. The Valley lies above the populous and industrious town of Huddersfield which has always been thirsty – as much because of the copious requirements of its textile industries as because of the needs of its citizens. As a result it has what must be one of the highest densities of reservoirs in the country – there are fourteen substantial ones in the Valley, and many more

FIG. 81.
Butterley Reservoir on a winter afternoon.

FIG. 82.
Cupwith Reservoir.

mill dams and cisterns. Roughly half feed the canal, and half the general water supply. There is one, Cupwith, that does neither.

Cupwith Reservoir

As textile production began to move from the domestic system to the factory system in the eighteenth century some of the earliest mills in the Colne Valley were built in Merrydale, the side valley that runs North-west from Slaithwaite up towards Bradshaw and the moors. It was owners of those early mills who petitioned the Earl of Dartmouth at the beginning of the nineteenth century to dam the Bradley Clough brook at Cupwith and create a holding reservoir that would regulate their water supply (Beaumont, 1985).

Cupwith is an atmospheric place, sitting below Cupwith Hill at a high edge of the valley. At an elevation of 1250 feet it is not visible from afar, but it is a place from which to appreciate the Valley's relationship with the moors above, with views from March Haigh Hill round to Pule Hill and along the southern watershed.

The feeder reservoirs for the canal

When the Huddersfield Canal was first proposed towards the end of the eighteenth century there was some ambivalence amongst the mill owners along the valley. They knew that a canal would provide the new, high volume, transport system they needed – the benefits of earlier schemes the other side of the Pennines and elsewhere in the West Riding were already apparent. But the processes of washing, fulling, and dyeing wool in their mills needed a generous water supply, and that came from the River Colne and its tributaries. They feared their supplies would be diverted to feed the canal. Their support for the construction of the canal was thus conditional on the creation of a system of new reservoirs to provide a separate source for the volumes needed to work the locks. The Huddersfield Canal Act of 1793 required reservoirs capable of providing 20,000 locks-full of water, at 180 cubic yards a time. No water was to be taken from the river.

Several of the reservoirs built to feed and regulate the water supply for the canal are, like Cupwith, high on the moors: March Haigh above the Owlers, Redbrook close to the turnpike routes below Thieves Bridge, and Black Moss and Swellands which sit next to each other on the moor between the Wessenden Valley and Standedge. The Black Moss reservoir lies across

FIG. 83.
March Haigh – a canal feeder reservoir on the tops.

the watershed and sluices allow it to feed either Swellands and thus the canal through the Colne Valley, or Brun Clough reservoir which sits just to the West of the Standedge cutting and deep below, just on the Saddleworth side of the canal summit.

You have to climb to the highest ground to see Cupwith, March Haigh, Swellands and Black Moss, but Redbrook Reservoir is more prominent and nodal at the head of the valley. It lies on the line of the turnpikes and the Roman road, and is adjacent to the Pule Holes shaft that drops down to the railway tunnel. A further three reservoirs were built close to the line of the canal itself, at Hill Top in Slaithwaite, at Sparth, and at Tunnel End, The last has long been silted up to form an area of wetland, but the other two are still prominent on the valley floor.

Water supply

To return to the famous extract from Defoe's 1724 record of his journey down into the Yorkshire communities to the East of the Pennines:

> ... As our road passed among them, wherever we passed any house we found a rill or gutter of running water ...

Whilst the scattered houses on the hillsides operated within a domestic textile and farming economy, the rills, gutters, springs and troughs provided an ample supply of water. It was sweet enough for household use, and soft enough for washing wool and cloth lengths. They are still there. Troughs gouged from large blocks of millstone are to be found close to the houses on the hillside, small streams are often in sight and earshot, and many have been carefully channelled to provide what would once have been the only water supply to the scattered houses along the hillsides.

But the coming of the factory system, and the rapid growth of Huddersfield and the villages along the floor of the Colne Valley which accompanied the building of more, and larger, mills led to a demand for a dependable high-volume water supply, and that required reservoirs. The early example of the Cupwith Reservoir feeding Merrydale, mentioned above, was built in the late eighteenth century, but the main period of dam building came fifty years later. Seven were built in the Colne Valley during a period of seventy years from 1836 to 1906. They were responses to the continuing struggle to keep ahead of demand. That story is set out by T.W. Woodhead in his *History of the Huddersfield Water Supplies* (1939).

For a while the increased demand in Huddersfield itself was met by a supply taken from the Colne at Folly Hall, using a water wheel constructed in 1743 by the Ramsden Estate at what is still known as Engine Bridge. The water was pumped to a cistern and from there distributed through the town.

FIG. 84.
One of many water troughs in the Valley. This one is at Bradshaw (SE 0494 1438).

But that proved wholly inadequate as industrial development accelerated and, as importantly, the industrial developments upstream meant that the supply became more and more polluted. Woodhead tells of the letter written by a Wakefield manufacturer who, complaining of the state of the water flowing down the Calder, using a pen dipped in the river as a source for his ink.

In 1826 Sir John Ramsden was petitioned with the request that

> ... an abundant and never failing supply of pure water might be obtained and conveyed to the town at a moderate expense.

An Act establishing the Huddersfield Water Commissioners, a sizeable group of 120 responsible citizens, was passed in 1827.

The Commissioners' first reservoir was constructed just beyond the watershed of the valley above Golcar: the Longwood Lower Reservoir was completed in 1828 with a capacity of 20 million gallons. But within the decade it was already proving an inadequate response. In the 1840s water supply to the town was being restricted to two days a week. Longwood Upper Reservoir followed, completed in 1848 with a capacity of 50 million gallons. That too was not enough to keep up with the demands of a town at the heart of the industrial revolution. The population of the town increased tenfold in the nineteenth century.

By the 1840s the first of the general water supply reservoirs for the Colne Valley itself, the Wessenden Reservoir, had been built by a separate set of commissioners empowered by an Act of 1836.

The next in the Valley were proposed in an 1865 report prepared by Colonel T.P.Crosland on behalf of the Huddersfield Commissioners as they struggled to keep up with demand. He set out a case for reservoirs at Blackmoorfoot and at Deer Hill.

But by then confidence in dam building had been knocked by a sequence of catastrophic failures, including two in the immediate area. The first Swellands dam broke in November 1810, sweeping six people to their deaths. A much bigger loss of life, more than eighty deaths, occurred in February 1852 when the Bilberry dam above Holmfirth burst. Slightly further away, more than 240 were killed in March 1864 when the Dale Dyke Dam near Sheffield burst. Understandably, those living underneath other recently built dams were fearful. Dorothy Beaumont's extracts from the Dartmouth Estate records include a note of the concerns of Slaithwaite residents:

> ... a general alarm throughout the village whenever any great quantity of water falls that the head of a very large Reservoir made by the Canal Company above the town [i.e. Hilltop Reservoir] will give way, which, if it should, there is no doubt that most of the houses in the village would be destroyed. ... it is certainly with great reason, an object of dread to most of them.

FIG. 85.
*Hill Top reservoir, sitting
above the centre of Slaithwaite.*

It may have been partly the then widespread concerns over the safety of reservoir dams that meant that a bid to extend the powers of the Huddersfield Waterworks Commissioners, and to enable the building of a dam at Blackmoorfoot, failed to pass when it was moved in the Commons in 1866.

The demand for water and the setbacks of the Waterworks Commissioners were significant factors in the reawakened drive to create the Huddersfield Corporation, which was established, rather belatedly in comparison to those of similar towns, in 1868. In his submission in support of the Bill, the Huddersfield Improvement Commissioners' Clerk, Joseph Batley, argued that the greater powers sought through incorporation, were required:

> … especially with a view to secure further supplies of water, the existing supplies thereof having latterly been found very defective. (Griffiths, ed., 2018)

The new Corporation bought out the interests of the Waterworks Commissioners and moved quickly to implement Colonel Crosland's proposals. The development of Deer Hill reservoir was underway by 1870. Blackmoorfoot followed a year later.

Like many of the canal feeder reservoirs, Deer Hill and Blackmoorfoot sit high on the valley sides. Deer Hill is at an elevation of 1150 feet, with little but the ganister quarries of Shooters Nab above it. Blackmoorfoot is a little lower (860 feet) but viewed from across the valley seems to sit on top of the

FIG. 86.
Blackmoorfoot – a reservoir that seems to sit on top of a hill.

FIG. 87.
The cut-off catchment that feeds Deer Hill reservoir.

ridge that separates Linthwaite from Meltham. Neither seems to have an extensive natural water catchment above it.

In fact both are dependent for their water feeds on two long catchment conduits, one above the other, that follow contours West along the side of the Valley and then South along the side of the Wessenden valley. For Blackmoorfoot there is a second cut-off conduit that skirts the western edge of Meltham. They seem an expensive means of accumulating a water supply, both in the costs of their initial construction and in their maintenance, but they are evidently effective, and they add a further line of high quality engineering to the Valley, high above the canal, railway and turnpikes.

Huddersfield Corporation went on to take over the first Wessenden Reservoir, and to build a further three up the side valley. The highest, known as Wessenden Head Reservoir, was constructed in 1876. Blakeley Reservoir, although authorised in an act of 1871, was not completed until 1904. The lowest and largest in the run, just above Marsden, is Butterley, finished in 1906.

By the turn of the century the Corporation had provided a supply of 500 million gallons to the town. It went on developing further sources, drilling bore holes at Wessenden Head, Blackmoorfoot, and near Nont Sarah's above Pole Moor. It acquired Deanhead reservoir in the Scammonden

FIG. 88.
*Wessenden Valley reservoirs:
Blakeley in the foreground,
Butterley below.*

Valley in 1913 and, as one of its final major capital schemes, it constructed Scammonden Reservoir itself, alongside the M62, in 1970. By the end of the nineteenth century it had also laid 240 miles of mains, and built cisterns above the settlements along the valley sides. Woodhead (1939) points out that the cistern above Scapegoat Hill, for instance, is fed from the Wessenden reservoirs, some seven miles away and on the other side of the valley. There can be few local authorities that have been as ambitious, as diligent, and ultimately as successful in investing in water supply.

Water plays a double role in the landscape. It draws and satisfies the eye, but is also bears witness to the nature and history of the Valley.

The visual effect is often to bring a focus and identity to the view. Many of the Valley reservoirs are high on the tops, where the moorland is a an expansive spread of peat, cotton grass and heather. It can seem featureless – but for a reservoir in the middle distance. Each sits differently in its relationship to the land and the waterways, streams or culverts, that feed it. Each catches the light in its own way. Each has its own shape, and each is a point of reference for any journey over the Valley's watersheds.

Collectively, they connect the landscape to the circumstances that have created it as a whole. In part the circumstances are those defined by its climate and geomorphology: the Colne Valley's abundant rainfall and underlying rock strata that ensure a high level of surface run-off. In part they are the economic and social history that created first the domestic economy of textiles and pastoral farming, and then the extraordinary growth of the West Riding's industry during the nineteenth century. Both needed water in large quantities. The troughs, sluices, conduits and reservoirs are witnesses to that history.

FIG. 89.
The elegant new sluice below the first Wessenden dam (SE 0567 0871).

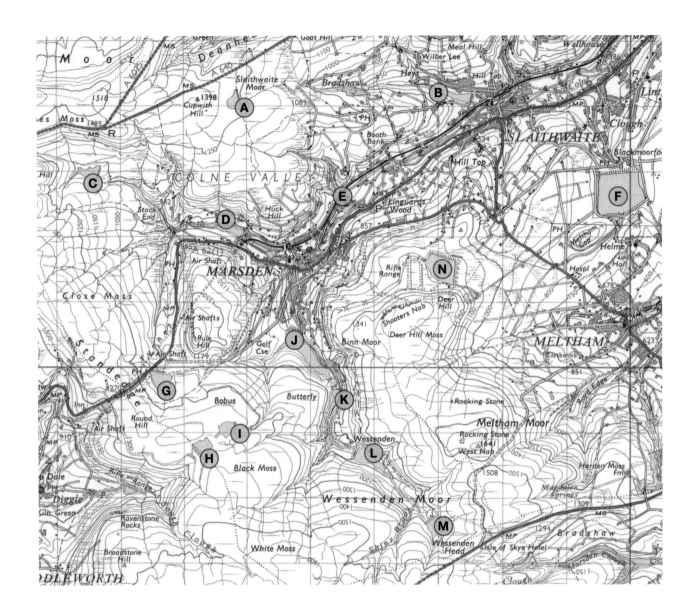

FIG. 90.

Locations of Reservoirs

A Cupwith
B Hill Top
C March Haigh
D Tunnel End
E Sparth
F Blackmoorfoot
G Redbrook

H Black Moss
I Swellands
J Butterley
K Blakeley
L Wessenden
M Wessenden Head
N Deer Hill

WEAVING
THE THREADS

THE SEPARATE SECTIONS of this text have considered individual elements of the Colne Valley landscape: water, tracks, chapels, settlements, quarries, walls, and fields.

They provide a series of filters through which to see what is in view as you stand on the hillsides and look around. Each helps define the Valley as a place which is distinct and itself. Once you have stood and stared about you in the Colne Valley its form and features become deeply engraved in the memory.

The elements are also threads. The text teases them out, and each can then be used to follow the story of how the landscape we see came to be. Part of the appeal of the Valley is the elemental strength of that story. The history of its development provides for a relatively straightforward narrative. Its chapters are legible in the Valley as it is today. They trace the making of a landscape that goes back further than is at first apparent, to the vaccaries of the thirteenth century, and the faint line of the Roman road.

But the threads are not really separate. They need to be made back into one cloth. It is woven together that they have created a Colne Valley landscape that, although rarely conventionally pretty or beautiful, is strong and purposeful, often handsome, and sometimes visually stunning.

The introduction to this text pays tribute to W.G. Hoskins, the historian whose book, *The Making of the English Landscape*, has inspired many subsequent studies of particular landscapes, including this one. Hoskins likened the broad sweep of a landscape in view to a symphony. The music can be enjoyed for its overall swell and emotional effect, but he encourages attention to the symphony's components:

> ... if instead of hearing merely a symphonic mass of sound, we are able to isolate the themes as they enter, to see how one by one they are intricately woven together and by what magic new harmonies are produced, perceive the manifold subtle variations on a single theme, however disguised it may be, then the total effect is immeasurably enhanced. So it is with landscapes of the historic depth and physical variety that England shows almost everywhere.

The landscape of the Colne Valley is captured in those words. It engages and moves anyone who looks around them on its hillsides, and it is generous in the rewards it offers to those whose curiosity leads them to unravel the story of its making.

REFERENCES

PUBLISHED

Ahier, Philip (1933), *The Halls in the Colne Valley* (Huddersfield, Advertiser Press)

Beaumont, Dorothy (1985), *Notes on the Dartmouth Estate* (Unpublished manuscript held by West Yorkshire Archive Service, catalogue number KC161/3)

Bower, D. and Knight, J. (1987), *Plain Country Friends: The Quakers of Wooldale, High Flatts and Midhope* (Wooldale, Meeting of the Religious Society of Friends)

Brunskill, R.W. (1971), *An Illustrated Handbook of Vernacular Architecture* (London, Faber)

Burnett, John; Vincent, David; and Mayall, David (1984), *The Autobiography of the Working Class: An Annotated Critical Bibliography, vol. 1: 1790-1900* (New York University Press)

Crump, W.B. (1938), 'The Little Hill Farm' *(Transactions of the Halifax Antiquarian Society)*

Crump, W.B. (1949), *Huddersfield Highways down the ages* (Huddersfield, Tolson Memorial Museum)

Crump, W.B., and Ghorbal, Gertrude (1935), *History of the Huddersfield Woollen Industry* (Huddersfield, Tolson Memorial Museum)

Davies, Richard; Petford, Alan; and Senior, Janet (Eds.) (2011) *The diaries of Cornelius Ashworth 1782 to 1816* (Hebden Bridge Local Historical Society)

Defoe, Daniel (1724), *A tour thro' the whole Island of Great Britain* (edition published by Peter Davies, 1927)

Ellis, Trevor (2017), *The Standedge Tunnels* (Huddersfield Canal Society)

Faull, M. L. and Moorhouse, S. A. (Eds) (1981), *West Yorkshire: An Archaeological Survey to A.D. 1500* (Wakefield, West Yorkshire Metropolitan County Council)

Fox, Michael and Fox, Peter (1991), *Pennine Passage* (Huddersfield Canal Society)

Griffiths, David (Ed) (2018), *Making up for lost time - the pioneering years of Huddersfield Corporation* (Huddersfield Local History Society)

Heaton, Herbert (1965), *The Yorkshire Woollen and Worsted Industries: From the Earliest Times to the Industrial Revolution* (Oxford, Clarendon Press)

Heaton, Herbert (1914), *The Letter Books of Joseph Holroyd (cloth-factor) and Sam Hill (clothier)* (Edition published by Halifax County Borough)

Heaton, William (1857), *The Old Soldier; the Wandering Lover and other poems* (Simkin)

Heginbottom J.A. (1993), 'Fences and fields: evolution of the Calderdale rural landscape from prehistoric times to the current day', *Proceedings of Halifax Antiquarian Society.*

Hey, David (2001), *Packmen, Carriers & Packhorse Roads* (Landmark Publishing)

Historic England (2017), *Agricultural Buildings Listing Selection Guide.*

Hobsbawm, Eric (1962) *The Age of Revolution: Europe 1789 – 1848* (Weidenfeld and Nicolson)

Hoskins, William George (1955), *The Making of the English Landscape* (London, Hodder & Stoughton)

Hulbert, Rev. Charles Augustus (1864), *Annals of the Church in Slaithwaite* (London, Longman and Co) (Accessible on Huddersfield Exposed website)

Jennings, B. et al (1992), *Pennine Valley: a history of Upper Calderdale* (Smith Settle)

Johnson, David (2016), *Quarrying in the Yorkshire Pennines – an Illustrated History* (Stroud, Amberley Publishing)

Keevill, Graham (1986), *Standedge Guide, 1986* (Kirklees MBC)

Lunn, Norman; Crosland, Bill; Spence, Bromwell; and Clay, Granville (2008) *The Romans came this way* (Huddersfield and District Archaeological Society)

Peck, Edward (1812), *The Life of John Metcalfe* (Published by Edward Peck)

Petch, James A. (1924), *Early Man in the District of Huddersfield* (Huddersfield, Tolson Memorial Museum)

Price, Dr. Richard (1780), *Essay on the Population of England* (Quoted in Rennie, Brown and Shirreff, 1794)

Raistrick, Arthur (1946), *Story of the Pennine Walls* (Dalesman)

Raistrick, Arthur (1970), *The West Riding of Yorkshire: Making of the English Landscape Series* (London, Hodder & Stoughton)

Rennie, Brown and Shirreff (1794) *General view of the Agriculture of the West Riding of Yorkshire* (W. Bulmer and Co.)

Seidel, Hazel (2013), *Laithes and Looms, Cows and Combsticks* (Marsden History Group)

Smith, A.H. (1963), *The place-names of the West Riding of Yorkshire* (English Place Names Society, vol 30-37)

Spikins, J.A. (2003), *Prehistoric People of the Pennines : Reconstructing the Lifestyles of Mesolithic Hunter-gatherers on Marsden Moor.* (West Yorkshire Archaeological Service and National Trust)

Stock, John (1874), *History of the Baptist Congregational and independent Church, Salendine Nook* (Elliot Stock) (Accessible on the Huddersfield Exposed website)

Sykes, D.F.E. (1906), *History of the Colne Valley* (Slaithwaite, F.Walker)

Sykes, D.F.E.(1908), *Miriam* (Re-published by Good Press, 2020)

Sykes. D.F.E. and Walker, C.H.(1898), *Ben O'Bills The Luddite* (Huddersfield, Advertiser Press)

Thompson, E.P. (1963), *The Making of the English Working Class* (London, Penguin Books)

Thomson, F.M.L. and Turner, M.(1978), *A study of the 1801 crop returns for England* (SSRC)

Tymon, Alison (2013), *Rocks and Landscapes of Marsden* (West Yorkshire Geology Trust)

West Yorkshire Joint Services (2017), *West Yorkshire Historic Landscapes Characterisation Project, Kirklees,* Historic Environment Record, PRN 4916

Whyte, Ian (2003), *Transforming Fell and Valley. Landscape and Parliamentary Enclosures in North West England* (University of Lancaster, Centre for North West Regional Studies)

Williams, Michael (1970), 'The Enclosure and Reclamation of Waste Land in England and Wales in the Eighteenth and Nineteenth Centuries', *Transactions of the Institute of British Geographers, vol 51*

Williamson, T.(2002), *The Transformation of Rural England: farming and the landscape 1700 -1870* (University of Exeter Press)

Wilson, Benjamin (1887), *The Struggles of an old Chartist* (Halifax, John Nicholson)

Woodhead, T.W.(1939) *History of the Huddersfield Water Supplies* (Huddersfield, Tolson Memorial Museum)

ONLINE RESOURCES

Atkinson, Christopher (2017) *Wessenden Valley Woodland Project: An Archaeological Desk Based Assessment* (Report commissioned by The Woodland Trust and Yorkshire Water, available at www.celebrate-our-woodland.co.uk)

Historic Ordnance Survey Maps, available from the National Library of Scotland website: https://maps.nls.uk/os/

A History of Launds Inn, on Rochdale Road above Clough Head, to be found at www.laundsinnmuseum.co.uk

Huddersfield Exposed: a collection of articles and pages about the history of Huddersfield and the surrounding area, to be found at: https://huddersfield.exposed/wiki/Welcome

Roman Roads Research Association, *The Roads of Roman Britain - a Gazetteer*, at roadsofromanbritain.org/index.html

UNPUBLISHED

'Hey Farms near Linthwaite', 18th century map, Special Collections, Brotherton Library, University of Leeds. Catalogue number YAS/MD358

Court Rolls of Slaithwaite cum Lingards, translated by Freeman, Margaret and Freeman, Mary. Unpublished document held by West Yorkshire Archive Service (Kirklees)

Smith, Nigel (2013) 'Settlements and Field Patterns in the South Pennines: a critique of morphological approaches to landscape history in upland areas' (Ph.D. thesis, University of Lancaster)

Tomlinson, Milner, 'Landlord Promotion of Agrarian Improvement in a Pennine Valley 1843 – 1853' (Unpublished essay)

Walker, Arthur (2018), *Author's notes from conversation with Arthur Walker, lifelong resident of Clough Head*

INDEX OF PLACES